My Life with Him:
Chicago Police Officer Clifton P. Lewis

EOW: December 29, 2011

To Those That Love Us

To GOD I give thanks, for giving me the strength to endure and to continue living, loving and speaking as he has put me here to do.

To my son Keyonta, through it all you have been my strength and I don't know what I'd do without you.

To My parents Corine Booker-Jackson, and Ronald Tucker Sr. Thank you for the gift of life and rearing me to be the woman that I am today.

To my "other" daddy's James L. Gardner and Teron Jackson your love and support is endless and forthcoming.

To Mrs. Maxine Johnson-Hooks, I call you "mom or "mama" because that is the honor that you have given to me. Not only because of the wonderful man that you raised and shared with me, but because you believed and had faith in me to embrace and cherish the heart of your son so I am very proud to be your "daughter".

To the Tactical team and the men and women of the 15th district Chicago Police Department, Superintendent Gary McCarthy, Commander Barbara West, Mayor Rahm

Emanuel, Carla, Peggy, Jimmy, Assasta and the rest of my CPD family; there are no words that can express the gratitude that I have for you. You were there for our family in our time of need and have stood by us every day after as well. You took me in as one of your own even though I didn't wear a badge, nor did I tackle the streets of Chicago, for this I thank you from the depths of my heart.

To my sisters Nicole, Matasha and Lashana, Clifton never told me that I would embrace such wonderful women. You are stuck with me for life and I want you to know that I love you ladies more than you'll ever know.

To his heart and mine Simone. Thank you for sharing your dad with me and allowing me to be a part of your life. Let's keep his legacy alive together.

To my cousin Lamesia, thanks for coming to get <u>ME</u> that night, if it wasn't for you this would not have been possible!

To those that I did not mention, I have not, nor will I ever forget that you have all played a wonderful and everlasting part of my life. I love you all for what you have done, for what you will do and for what's to come.

MEETING HIM

I NEVER thought that I would date again after coming out of a 9 year relationship that broke me, pulled me and damaged my heart, yet taught me a lesson. I had so many thoughts and feelings racing through my mind. That's it I am done with this relationship shit, I don't have time to play games, I don't want my heart balled up and stomped on any more. With all of these thoughts my mind was made up, I would never date again and all of my time would be devoted to raising my son and taking care of ME!

All of that changed one November night. I went along with my cousin Lamesia to help get her car back, but in order for us to get it back "legally" we had to call the police for assistance. My mind wasn't on the "police" I told my cousin that our mission was to get her car back even if I had to hot wire it myself. But she insisted that we wait for the police and today and for the rest of my life I am SO glad we did. We were standing outside my car that fall night and as we waited this police car pulls up. With a tire iron in hand I told my cousin "That might be the police that's going to help us, let me find out". So I walked across the street to where the police car was parked. The officer was looking down I guess doing paper work and as I approached I said to myself "OH MY GOD he is fine". I found myself getting a little excited and praying that when I approached this car and look down at his hands there wouldn't be a ring on his finger. Now mind you I still had the tire iron in my hand but none of that mattered, all I could think about was this officer that came to assist us.

As I approached the car the officer kind of looked up and at my hand and slowly said "May I help you?" while still looking at my hand. I wanted to say out loud YES YOU CAN but I wasn't thinking about the kind of help that he was talking about so I had to catch myself and remember the reason for me walking over to the police car in the beginning. After gaining my composure I asked the officer "Are you the responding officer that will be assisting us in getting a car back?" He looked up over his glasses and said "Yes I am". I immediately got that feeling of excitement all over again. I ran back over to my cousin and said to her "Girl he is here to help us get your car back, and if he gets out of that car and he is taller than me (which is anything over 5'4) I am asking for his number". My cousin turned to me and said "No you not because you don't do stuff like that and plus we are here to get my car back not you getting the hook up". Please believe that everything she said went into one ear and out of the other. But she did have a good point, because I would never approach a guy and ask for his number but it was something about this guy that made me flip my own script. I was determined to get his number no matter what. Of course I still had the real reason for the officer coming to assist us somewhere in my mind, really I did!

So I waited patiently for him to get out of the car, I waited and waited and finally he got out. I didn't actually see him get out of the car at first because one of my cousins kids tapped on the window to ask me a question. So while tending to my cousin's baby answering the question that was asked I turned around and the officer that was sitting in the car was now walking towards us and in amazement I looked up and said "OH MY GOD I said wanted him to be tall but I wasn't talking 6 feet 6 inches tall". After starring at him I snapped out of the trance he had me in and said "Hello" when he spoke back I could have passed out. This man's voice was deep and serious, but sexy. At this point I wanted to do all the talking but I didn't know any of the information that he needed so I just started off by saying "It's her car that we need your assistance with" then I grabbed my cousin and told her "Girl I got to have his number, I have to get his number". As he was speaking to my cousin taking her information I was completed dazed by this man's presence not only did he look good in his uniform but his body, voice, and psychical attractiveness pulled me like a string of a yo-yo. My mind started racing and thoughts kept popping up, "Damn girl what are you waiting on, you want him so what's taking you so long to ask for his number, ok scary ass just ask the question are you married and if not will you marry me". After minutes and minutes of talking to myself I finally got the courage to walk over to him and said "I usually don't do this and I know that you are working right now but can I please have your number?" My cousin face had this look of surprise on it and after a minute or two she said to the officer "Look why don't you write your number down and I'll give you her number, because I don't think she realize that I am trying to get my car back".

I know at this point he thought I was crazy and the look he gave me actually said what he didn't want to say to my face. "She has to be out of her mind if she thinks that I am giving her my number. She has to be crazy still standing there holding a damn tire iron in her hand in front of the police". He continued to talk to my cousin and after about 3 minutes he walked back over to his squad car and yes like a stalker I politely followed because I was determined to get his number.

Yes he noticed that I was following him and yes I noticed that I had that DAMN tire iron still in my hand. He stopped me and said "Excuse me miss, but can I ask what do you plan to do with that tire iron in your hand?" I looked down and said "oh... um if I tell you will you lock me up?" He kind of smiled and said

"It all depends". I was a little scared but I told the truth which was "If my cousin's crazy ass boyfriend came out that house and tried anything I was going to bust his damn head". He smiled a little and said "Naw I won't lock you up as long as you don't do it in front of me". I know that he was lying but still a sigh of relief came over me along with lust because that's exactly what I was doing while talking to this officer. He continued to do his work and I continued to work on getting his number. I asked over and over again until he finally said "You are serious", and I said "YES I AM" and I pulled out my cell phone and said 773, 708 (area codes) he just smiled and continued working. I don't think he understood how serious I was. I was not leaving unless I had his number.

When my cousin went over to her car I went over to the officer's car and said "I was truly serious about your number, so is it a possibility that I can have it?" He looked up at me over his glasses and said 773 my body started tingling and that excitement that I spoke of earlier reached the ultimate level. After all of my begging and pleading I got OFFICER'S LEWIS's number. I skipped back over to my cousin like I was a 3 year old just leaving the candy store but the entire woman that I am was smiling from ear to ear. I forgot about my cousin's crazy ass boyfriend and yes I finally dropped the tire iron. I thanked my cousin over and over for asking me to come with her. I also threw in her face the fact that I got his number and she said that I wouldn't. My cousin was tickled and said to me "I can't believe you did it I am so happy for you, but is it okay for him to finish up with me so I can get my car and my kids home. I laughed and said "girl yeah I got what I wanted so he can do whatever".

Officer Lewis completed what he had to finish in order for my cousin to take her car. When he was done he walked over to me and asked if he could tell me something. Me smiling trying to act like I wasn't nervous said "sure". He looked down at me (because that how tall he was over me) and said "To be honest with you I was actually going to ask you for your number. I think you're cute, crazy but a very nice looking lady". Again trying to keep my composure but all jittery inside I said "Thanks and me being all persistent only came from me seeing something that I liked". Then I asked "When can I call you"? And he said "Whenever you like". From that moment on, began the start of my EVERYTHING, my LIFE, my HAPPINESS. I don't know why but I started to feel different, but it was a good kind of different. That may sound crazy, but I think this was GOD's plan.

Later on that evening I received a text message from Officer Lewis which stated "It really was a pleasure meeting you this evening, although you held on to that tire iron for a long time LOL. I hope that you have a good evening and I hope to talk to you soon". Well soon was 10 minutes after I got that text message. I really wanted him to know that I was so serious about him but at the same time I didn't want to seem overzealous. I don't know what it was that had me so attracted to Officer Lewis. It wasn't his profession didn't care about that; it wasn't the fact that he didn't lock my ass up for threatening to bust some body's damn head (thanked GOD for that). I think that it was his stern assertiveness yet gentle persona. No matter what it was I was extremely happy and for the first time I forgot about my initial plan of never dating again.

A couple of days went pass and Officer Lewis or should I say Clifton and I talked on the phone and decided that we should do breakfast. I was really interested and eager to find out what he was like out of uniform, what his everyday life was like outside of being one of Chicago's finest.

We had our first of many breakfast dates at IHOP. To be honest I was the one who chose IHOP. I wanted to be in a neutral but natural environment plus I had plenty to say and a lot to ask and I had a taste for some pancakes and harsh browns. I am one who believes in old sayings especially the one "Let the gentleman pay for the meal," but at the same time I am also a firm believer that a lady should always keep a little change just in case something strange should occur and it was a week before my pay day so my funds were limited to the IHOP menu prices and CTA bus fare.

At breakfast Clifton was quiet and reserved I did most of the talking. I started off by asking him how long had he been a policemen, we talked about our kids, my son Keyonta who was about 9 at the time, and his daughter Simone who was 3. He then asked me how long had I been on my job and was I always so aggressive when it came to certain things like the incident with my cousin or asking someone for their phone number. I told him no; I am not always like that I just hated my cousin boyfriend because of the things he did to her and the way he treated her. I am not a confrontational person at all but when you mess with my family I will go there. As for his phone number I had to do whatever it took to get it.

Our conversation started off well but I think Clifton went into shock when I openly laid a lot of "first" on the table. The first thing that I told him was that I was not looking to cash in on his 401k because I had my own, I didn't care about his bank account, because I also had one of those as well. I told him that I was looking for someone who respects me for who I am, who is willing to accept and respect my son and someone who wants a drama free, fun and a long term relationship. Clifton had this look on his face like "WOW" did she just lay out a pre-nup on our first date? Well if that's what he was thinking, than yes that's exactly what I did.

I had to put everything on the table with Clifton because I was at a point in my life where it was all about me and my son but I knew that I didn't want to be alone and I also knew that I didn't want someone who was going to put me through heart ache again, plus I figured laying all of this on him at one time gave me the chance to see what I was dealing with. Either the gentleman was going to stay and begin to work on building a life together or Clifton would say thanks but no thanks and go about his business. With all that said, Clifton didn't leave so I'm guessing that we had the same thing in mind or breakfast was just that good and he was being polite and after breakfast I wouldn't get a phone call ever again.

Overall I was really enjoying myself with Cliff. He didn't have a law enforcement vibe he was really relaxed and "allowed" me to continue to do all of the talking. I really grab his undivided attention when I asked him was he seeing someone else. His eyes kind of opened a little more and he took a huge sip of his ice tea then he asked "What made you say that"? I paused for a moment because I wanted to laugh but I didn't. My reply was "because I don't believe in sharing and if I have to share you then I don't want you". I had to apologize for being so blunt about it but at the same time I had to keep it real with him. He looked at me with a small smile and said "I feel you" and no I am not seeing anyone else. That brought a smile to my face and I can honestly say that I believed him, but I don't know why.

Breakfast was enjoyable and he did pay for our meal and he also left the tip. After breakfast we went back to his place which was a nice one bedroom. Yes you knew that he was a bachelor or "a single man" because that's what his apartment reflected; weights, TV, a couch and a cat. He was a gentleman the whole time.

While we were there things kind of changed from breakfast. He asked me questions, but more opened ended questions. We talked about pervious relationships and we found out that we both had experiences that we did not want to relive again. I expressed to Clifton that the only thing I was looking for in a relationship was trust, understanding, fun, and of course great intimacy. (And with him that soon followed). He laughed and sort of touched on what he was looking for in a relationship as well. He told me that many of his so called relationships were not considered "serious". He wasn't the type that made issues out of everything; he just wanted to be with someone who accepted him and his daughter and that he was also looking for someone who wasn't a nagger and needy. Someone who wasn't a drama queen, and who wasn't a disrespectful, self centered female that only thought of herself. I felt everything he said but it was something about that word "needy" that didn't sit so right with me so I had him explain what "needy" meant and for him to give me a sense of what he considered self-centered. I had a clue about the disrespectful part.

Cliff told me that needy was just that "needy" always having your hand out instead of giving, always expecting for him to do everything and someone who always complained about everything. I actually agreed with him 100% and had much respect for what he said because to be honest there are plenty of women who fit the description of everything he mentioned but I am so proud to say that I wasn't one.

After taking all of that in I told him that he didn't have to worry about my hand being out unless it was necessary for it to be out which meant that it would only be that way if I needed something and just didn't have the means of getting it myself. I also expressed to him that no relationship is ever going to be 50\50 sometimes it might be 60/40 even 90/10 but ours would never get to the point where we were taking advantage of one another. I have always worked for what I wanted and have never been the begging type and never will I be. Because no matter what neither myself nor my son would ever be without. I told him that he didn't have to worry about me disrespecting or mistreating his daughter because just like me I come as a package and that's how I felt about him. He took a sip of his ice tea that he brought home with him from breakfast and said to me "ok we'll see" and left it at that.

STILL NEW AND WORKING AT IT

Clifton and I were really enjoying each other. We got together whenever we could because of our work schedules. He had a varying schedule while I had a set work schedule. We did a lot of talking on the phone but again enjoyed being in each other presences. Our first outing where we actually saw more than an hour of one another was at an R. Kelly concert at the Chicago theatre and then dinner afterwards. He was always a gentleman. He opened the car door each time I got in or out, he made several compliments about the way I was dressed (of course I turned casual into casual sexy and if you are a woman you know exactly what I am talking about!). I believe in giving a taste of what's to come but making him wonder "if she looks like this in that, I can just imagine what she will look like in…" (Wait did I mention that Clifton met me in jogging pants and a tee-shirt).

Let me just say that Cliff paid for the concert tickets and dinner but he asked if I could leave a tip for our hostess afterwards, I guess he was testing me. I didn't mind or should I say I didn't have a problem with his little test so yes I did leave the tip. After dinner he asked if I would like to go back to his place and I said yes, again he was a true gentleman. When we got to his place we sat in the car for a minute to talk. The first thing that Clifton said to me was "I didn't ask you to come over tonight thinking anything was going to happen I just really enjoy your company and I don't or wouldn't have a problem if you want to go home". If this was game I will admit that his was good, but it wasn't he was truly genuine about what he said. I told him that if it's one thing that he had to remember about me it was this: I know how to speak my mind and if I am not comfortable doing something he would know about it. But I appreciated his honesty and I appreciated him giving me a choice. He smiled and said the second thing is "I don't think my cat likes it when you come over". With a small chuckle my response to that was "oh well she'll just have to deal with it, and I don't like her either but because I like her owner I'll put up with her" We got out of the car and went upstairs.

For some strange reason I had the worst headache so when we entered his apartment I literally sat on the couch and laid my head on the arm of it. He asked was I ok and I told him that I had a terrible headache but other than that I was good. He offered me some Advil and asked me if it was cool for him to check out the highlights on ESPN. I told him yes and then asked if it was cool if I lay across his lap.

    Believe me when I tell you, this man was so warm and compassionate. Nothing happen that night and just like he said neither one of us was expecting it to. It's just the thing of it though, some guys would have really expected and wanted **MORE** literally! Sorry if that offends anyone but fact is fact and truth is just that TRUTH! I awoke the next morning to breakfast (couldn't believe that) this man was really pouring it on and you better believe that I was taking all of it in. He asked me was I feeling better and asked if O.J was ok because that's all he had.

    I was now at the point where all I could do is smile; because for the first time in a while I was being treated like someone really appreciated me with no string attached. After breakfast he asked me if I had checked on my son to see if he was okay. (My God this man) I told him no but thanks for asking. He immediately handed me my cell phone and said "well you should call to see if everything is cool with him". In disbelief I did just what I was asked to do and yes my son was fine and so was I.

I really couldn't wrap my mind around him. First breakfast, my son, and then to top it off he was a gentleman the whole entire night. Ok I must admit and please don't judge me but laying next to him that night the thought's going through my mind were so **ADULT RELATED** that I should have been ashamed of myself but that's what happens when attraction arises. Trust me it wasn't HIM that I was worried about, it was ME. I was worried about touching him and he didn't make it easy either. We both showered but I threw on my PJ's (the huge oversized tee-shirt that he gave me) in the bathroom, but he walked into the bedroom with a bath towel on then asked me to rub some lotions on his back. While rubbing his back with lotion I started to have hot flashes, not the kind women get going through menopause. I had lusting, sexual related hot flashes especially when he "accidentally" dropped the towel that he had wrapped around him and I saw the package he was working with. All I could do to try to keep myself from jumping all over this man was to turn over and play "possum" and focus on the slight headache I had. But LORD HAVE MERCY! Is all that needed to be said.

I thanked him for breakfast and also thanked him for thinking about my son. All in all I had a wonderful first experience with Clifton and I was really looking forward to many many more. I asked him what his plans were for the day. He said that he was going to see his daughter later on that day but he had nothing else planned. So I said to him that since he cooked me breakfast maybe I could cook him dinner and we could grab some movies, but at my place this time. He agreed and that was that.

You never really think about first impression until you have experienced one like I did with Clifton. I was in awe all day after he dropped me off at home. I couldn't help but think about him and thank GOD for such a kind person. My hat went off to him first and foremost for asking about my son and making sure that I did what was right by him (checking in to make sure he was ok) I knew he was good because I would never leave my son with anyone that wouldn't take care of him but still Cliff at that time didn't know that so he made sure that I made sure my son was good and that was one of many things that drew me to Mr. Lewis. I had much respect for him because like me I loved my son and he loved his daughter and spoke of her often. I asked when I would get the chance to meet the little miss that he always spoke about, and his response was soon, real soon.

Unfortunately Clifton was unable to make it to dinner that night because he was called in to work. He did ask if he could stop by and take it to go and asked if he could get a rain check on the movie until the next time. I couldn't say no, so I agreed. He stopped by and got the plate. He asked what was on it and I said: Greens, baked chicken, mac and cheese, dressing and corn bread. He laughed and said "did you really cook all of this or did you mother help you?" I was offended of course but at the same time tickled. My reply was "NO!! My mother didn't help me and yes I cooked everything that's on your plate and as a matter of fact I cooked it from scratch NO box stuff"! (Ok the corn bread was JIFFY but everything else was from scratch HONESTLY) He said to me "yeah we will see but I must tell you that I really don't eat anybody's dressing except my mother's" and my response was "well that's not your mother's but I bet it's close to it so make sure you let me know".

Later on that night I'm thinking after he ate Clifton called me and said "Ms. Tucker I'll give it you, you hooked that up and yes I will call my mother to inform her that I found somebody that makes good dressing so I should be good for thanksgiving". Flattered for two reasons (1) I knew that he was going to enjoy it and (2) it was January and he's already speaking long range stuff. He even said that his partner asked what happen to his plate and he told him "she only made enough for me" which in turn came to be the saying every time dinner was made from there on out.

Months and months went by before I had the chance to meet the wonderful women in Clifton's life besides me of course. It was around April of 2005 when I finally had the opportunity to meet Clifton mother Mrs. Maxine Johnson-Hooks. He asked me if I would like to ride out to his mom house with him one afternoon and of course I jumped at the chance because as always he spoke so highly of her. He told me that if it wasn't for his mom he didn't know where he would be. He gave all the credit to his mother for the man that he turned out to be. (AND SO DO I) So I really wanted to meet the woman that he just adored and admired so much. Oh and I have to say in his words "she is my mama and I don't share her with anyone" (Sorry sis that's what he said!)

When we got to his mom's house he informed me that she had a dog but she was a good dog; what he didn't warn me about was how big her dog was. (For the record Clifton was an animal lover and so is just about everyone in his family). As we approached the door I stopped and said "I am not going in there" his mom's dog Ziu was standing at the door a big dark haired dog that had to be taller than me on all fours so I could just imagine what she looked liked if she was to jump up. Clifton smiled and said "you're good she won't bother you". Yeah right was all I was thinking. I have had some bad experiences with dogs so I didn't trust them. They could be the cutest, smallest dog ever but I still didn't trust them no matter what.

So after much debate I finally went in but behind him and very closely behind him I will say. Clifton grabbed her by her chain and said "good girl, she's alright you don't have to get her" First of all I didn't find that funny but I was so relieved when he took her outside. Ms. Hooks and I talked for a while; I told her how it was a pleasure to finally meet the woman that Cliff spoke so highly of. I also informed her of how I literally begged him to meet her and his response would always be "why do you want to meet my mother". She laughed and "said yeah that's him alright". As our conversation continued I told her that I was the only girl with 4 brothers with my mother and I had two sisters and 3 brother on my father's side and that I was the oldest out of us all and that I also had a son. She then went on to tell me that Clifton had an older brother that passed away named Michael. She also said that he and his sister Nicole literally fought like cats and dogs but at the end of the day they always told each other they loved one another.

Clifton came back into the house with Ziu. I don't know why but I thought she was coming straight towards me so I flinched a little and his mother said "oh its ok honey she won't bother you" and she told Clifton to chain her in the back until we left. Of course he had to be all smart about it, "girl stop being such a scary cat she ain't thinking about you." My response: "WHAT EVER" you don't know what she's thinking about. We stayed at his mom's house for a while and after being there for that short time I saw that Clifton was a "mama's boy" which I thought was cute. I didn't have a problem with that at all and in all honesty I hope that my son will be the same way. He asked several times if there was anything that she needed him to do before he left. As she gathered his mail she said "no dear, I can't think of anything that needs to be done but thank you".

As we departed I again told Cliff's mom that it was really a pleasure to meet her and I hope that this would be the first of many visit and she said likewise. (Note: 9 years later she's my mother-in-law whom I love very much). As we were leaving his mom's house he asked "so what did you two talk about"? I said why? Trust me I didn't ask any "how was Clifton as a child questions". He replied "Well it doesn't matter, I'll call my mama later and find out what you talked about and my mama will tell me". I couldn't do anything but laugh because as I stated earlier Clifton is a mama's boy and I actually believed that if he asked she would tell him something but not everything.

Every little thing that Clifton did impressed me more and more. There wasn't a time that he didn't make me smile and there wasn't a time that I thought of **NOT** being with him. Deep down inside I felt or was holding on to the fact that I could someday be Mrs. Clifton P. Lewis. But I knew I had a lot of work to do before I could even think about getting close to "I DO". I knew that Clifton was able to love and love hard but he had this brick wall up that was as tall as he was and the hardest thing for me was trying to tear it down.

Disbelief And No Explanation

About 6 months into our relationship still beaming on cloud nine and enjoying everything that entitled Cliff and Latrice Cliff told me that he was going out of town for the weekend to help a friend of his move and because I trusted him I didn't ask any question I just said ok. He gave me the keys to the car and his apartment and said to me "make sure to feed Fiona" (his cat) which he treated like a damn baby. I agreed and told him to have a safe trip. When he returned I still didn't go into questioning him about where the friend moved to or who the friend was because like I said I trusted him and was comfortable with his actions and or his decisions but sorry to say that all changed about 2 months later.

Let me just remind you of the statement that I made to Clifton on our first date. **"I don't share, and if I have to share you then I don't want you"**. Anyway an incident happened and

I found out a few things that really pissed me off to the point where I was ready to commit a crime against the police not all just one in particular.

I called Clifton out about this incident and it didn't surprise me when he denied it, that's just what I thought he would do because he got caught trying to play the field on both ends. Not to drag this any further I found out that the friend that Clifton helped move was a female and that while helping her move he also slept with her. A few people that I shared personal things with asked me how I knew or how did I find out? Well to answer that question I'll just say never let your girlfriend count your condoms and then unpack your travel bag to find a wrapper to one inside or let your girlfriend get a phone call from her doctor with her test results after her annual exam.

My heart dropped and my feelings were hurt. I sat in my car and cried not because of what I found out but because I led myself to believe that Clifton was different and that I trusted him. I pulled myself together and I called Clifton and went straight to the point. I really didn't give him a chance to say hello I snapped!

"WHO ELSE ARE YOU SLEEPING WITH?" His response to that was "Uh I'm good and what did you say?" I know like hell he heard everything I said but because he wanted to play dumb I played dump right along with him and I slowly said **"WHO ELSE ARE YOU SLEEPING WITH"?** Again he was like "Uh…why would you ask me something like that? Trying to hold back tears I told him "because you should have checked your damn bag before you brought it back home with you and asked me to grab something out of it. Then I asked him "so did you use the condom or did you have it "just in case"? At that moment I did cry. Clifton really couldn't talk because he was working. He asked me not to cry and that he would see me in a little while so we could talk about the situation.

Honestly I have never disrespected him or his job but I was so mad and hurt that at that moment I didn't care about him or his job. I told him that I wanted him to answer my question and I wanted an answer NOW! **What other female(s) are you sleeping with?** I guess he step out of the car because he said to me "only you" where is all of this coming from? I told him he was lying and I was done. Just as I was about to hang up the phone he said "wait Trice, ok you and her. (He did say her name but I won't). "Sweetheart where is all of this coming from"? Still crying I told him that I had just left my doctor's office concerning my test results of my recent annual exam and for the first time since I've been sexually active and sleeping with him one of my test results came back positive.

Of course he was in denial and said "that can't be possible" so I asked him was he calling me a lie? Or was he saying that I was the one sleeping around? My heart broke even more and again I told him that I was done. I just want the few things that I had at his apartment and I hope that he gets himself checked out, and then tell that nasty **Bitch** that he slept with to get her **nasty ass** checked to. (Please forgive my language but that's how I felt at the time).

I couldn't believe I was going through this. All this time I was placing him in a whole different category. His sincere, thoughtful, and caring ways was just bait to reel me in. This just brought me to the conclusion that he was no different from the rest and that my "happily ever after" was crushed.

Clifton called me back and apologized several times and asked if we could talk about it once he got off of work. I didn't want to talk I just wanted my few things and I was out. How could I have been so stupid? How did I forget that he was a man! I wanted with all my heart to be right, I wanted Clifton to be different I wanted him to be the one that changed my UNEASED position about men.

Confused and hurt I waited patiently for Clifton to get off of work. Hours passed and I had a chance to calm down and reflect on things. I won't lie and say that the news that my doctor gave me wasn't still playing over and over in my head but my heart was saying talk to him, listen to him and hear him out before you make a decision that you might regret. So I did. I listened to my heart and I gave Clifton the opportunity to explain himself. It was about Five O'clock in the evening when he called my phone and told me he was home. Still upset but listening to my heart I went to his apartment. As I asked him to do he put all of my things into a bag but before he gave them to me he asked if we could talk. I agreed and we talked. I don't know why I am always so emotional but it took everything in me to hold back the tears and my thoughts of stabbing him to.

Clifton admitted to me that he was wrong and that I had every right to be mad, upset, angry all of the above. He said that it was not his intention to sleep with this friend it just happened. I said to him "I hate those words it just happened. I don't believe in it just happened. Why is that always the fall on answer when someone FUCK'S up? I truly believe in it happened because you wanted it to happen". As we sat and talked I was quiet for a long time but all emotional, I asked Clifton why? Was the urge that strong? He couldn't have waited one more day until he came home? And if he couldn't why didn't he use the condoms that he packed? In disbelief he just sat with his head down while holding my hand and said "Trice I don't know".

Being who I am one half of me somewhat wanted to believe that he didn't know why he made such a fucked up mistake but the other half of me couldn't cope. I told Clifton that

I needed some time and that it would be best that we didn't see each other for a while. My throat had the biggest lump in it after saying those words to him because I knew that he was the one. This man was meant to be my husband and just like that I was walking away from him.

Clifton said that he didn't want that but with tears streaming down my face I grabbed my bag and I turned to him and said "stay sweet and make sure you get yourself checked out". Before I could leave out of the door Clifton grabbed me and hugged me and said "sweetheart I am sorry please don't leave this way and he wiped the tears that were falling down my face. Only GOD and I know how I wanted to stay and let him continue to hold me but I couldn't my stubbornness and hurt wouldn't let me.

After all of that Clifton and I didn't talk for about 3 weeks it was hard but I didn't break. My son would ask if I had talked to Cliff and I would just say no. Then Keyonta would say "well I saw him today or he was by my school and he asked about you". My response to that was a very dull "that's nice". As the days went by it turned into a month that I had not talk to Officer Lewis, he called me several times and each time I would tell my son to tell him that I wasn't home or I would just let the call go straight to voice mail.

The bible says "out of the mouth of a child" and this is so true. It was my son who said to me "mom you should talk to him he seems like a good guy and I like him". Why do you keep telling me to tell him that you are not here when he calls"? I was a little shocked and couldn't believe that my son of all people was saying this. It's rare that a "BOY" or in my son's case "a young man" accepts a man that's not his father to be with his mother. I couldn't tell my son why I didn't want to talk to Clifton but I did tell him that he was correct in saying that he was a good guy to kind of clear the air.

One evening while sitting at home with my son the phone rang I looked at the caller ID and saw that it said Lewis, Clifton I let it ring twice and on the third ring my son answered and said "hey Cliff" they held a conversation for a minute and then my son said "would you like to speak to my mom?" I am sitting looking at this kid shaking my head "NO why did you say that" and out of nowhere Keyonta said "mama talk to him he's been calling all day."

I took the phone and smiled at my son and said "I am going to get you". Calmly I said "hello" on the other end Clifton said "Hello Ms. Tucker how are you"? With a smirk I said I am fine Mr. Lewis how are you? He laughed and said "I am good; you aren't going to hang up on me are you"? Now I am thinking how did he know, but I said no and we conversated for a while. I won't elaborate too much on our conversation but I will say that he told me about another young lady that he asked out and how that went totally wrong. He then went on to ask me if I would go out to dinner with him because he missed hanging out with me.

Again here comes that stubborn side of me, I hesitated for a minute but yes finally came out of my mouth. We talk a while longer and Clifton told me that he was glad that I accepted his phone call and that he didn't like the fact that we hadn't talk in a while and that would never happen again. Of course I was thinking to myself "it's your fault" and I did miss talking to him too but I didn't let him know that. Before we got off the phone he said goodnight and asked me to tell my son thanks for looking out for him. It was really a pleasure talking to Clifton again I will admit that. I did miss him and wanted to talk to him way before then but I was still trying to get over being hurt and I just wasn't ready.

ON THE ROAD TO
Starting over

Preparing for my date with Clifton was fun. I went through a few outfits because I wanted this "first of second" impression to be on point. I wanted him to see what he was missing. Now I know of course that's being a little bitchy but hey he brought it on himself and I was having fun with it. I have never worn make up because I never thought I needed it, my beauty is pure inside and out but I will say that I wear some fierce lip gloss thanks to Victoria Secrets and that night these lips of mine were very kissable. My auntie Donnie had given me this beautiful white sweater so I wore that with my nicely fitting jeans and my heeled boots to match.

On most occasions Clifton was a stickler for time (I admit with laughter that we were almost never on time for anything) but this particular time when he said that he would be there at 7:30 he was there at 7:30.

When I got in the car he looked and smiled. Of course my little ego was "saying yeah he's loving what he's seeing". Like always he complemented me and said that he was glad to see me. Likewise I said and I also complemented him because the man was looking good. Clifton always kept his appearance up; I have to give him much respect for that.

To start off some form of conversation because we were both quiet for a while I asked how his mother and daughter were doing? He said they were good. I couldn't help but blush because he kept looking at me and smiling (one of the few times I got a smile out of him) I had to ask "why do you keep looking at me like that?" he said "no particular reason. I still can't believe that you wouldn't take my calls and you look really nice tonight". I laughed and told him that I liked the way he threw the "you didn't take my calls" into his complement.

As we were driving to our destination Clifton apologized again and told me that even if I didn't want to go out with him again after this, he still wanted me in his life and if it wasn't as his girl then being a good friend was cool.

Knowing how I felt about him, being just his friend was out of the question. I wanted to be his girlfriend; no wait actually I wanted to be his WOMAN! We were both passed the age of what I like to call the "boyfriend /girlfriend stage." It was hard as hell for me but I told Clifton that I accept his apology and that starting that night we would place all of what happen behind us and that I didn't just want to be his girlfriend I wanted to be his woman and one day his WIFE. He smiled and grabbed my hand and said "Trice I am sorry and thank you for coming out with me tonight" but he didn't comment on the "wife" word.

We saw a movie that night then went to dinner afterwards. He let me choose where we would have dinner so I chose the Longhorn Steak House. While at dinner we laughed and talked and joking he said "do you have a curfew"? I looked at him and said "it all depends". He replied "It all depends on what?

I didn't expect a comeback answer from him so fast so I said "no Mr. Lewis I do not have a curfew". "Good because I want you to go someplace else with me tonight" was his response. Wiping my mouth I said ok, but can I ask where? He said "NO". I like surprises but I wasn't too sure about this one because I had no idea what he had up his sleeve so I waited but constantly tried to make him give me a hint, a clue, something.

After dinner we drove for a while and I started to get a little impatient because I had no idea as to where we were going. Of course I started to think "is he taking me to some vacant lot where he could kill me and nobody could hear me scream for help" (yeah I watch a lot of TV). I asked Clifton were we lost because it seemed like we were driving in circles. He just looked at me and said no we're good. After about 10 more minutes of driving we finally reached out destination. As he was parking the car I looked at the sign to the building that we pulled up to and it said the **AMABIANCE INN and SUITES**. Clifton got out the car and said wait here I'll be right back.

As I wait for him to return my mind was running a thousand miles a minute. This was totally unexpected but in its own little way romantic but still I wondered what or who brought this to his attention and was I comfortable with being intimate with him again If intimacy was to take place. I knew for a fact that I was longing to be intimate with Clifton again but in the back of my mind I was still thinking should I be so quick to indulge?

Clifton returned to the car with keys in hand. I guess he noticed the expression on my face and he asked was I ok? Yes I am good I said. He then told me that one of his "friends" told him about this place and he wanted to check it out with his girl. I didn't go there by saying "which one" because that would have been wrong plus I was the one sitting next to him (but I was so tempted). Clifton got back out of the car and came around to my side and opened my door, he grabbed my hand and helped me out of the car.

When we got to the room I was very impressed. I turned to him and said "Cliff this is very nice". Our room was gorgeous.

It was a suite with stairs that led to king size bed and a beautiful fire place. He took my jacket and we sat and talked for a while. I told Clifton that I missed him and that I wanted this relationship and our friendship to work but I would not put up with being lied to, and that I was never ever going to **SHARE** him with another woman again and I meant that. I truly hope he was taking what I said to heart because I was only going to play the fool once. Clifton looked at me and said "Trice I am sorry. I was wrong and it will never happen again. I know right now it's hard for you to trust me or believe anything that I say but I want to be with you and I want our relationship and our friendship as well". He also said that he believed in and wanted a second chance. Then in the mist of all of that he said "Sweetheart is Keyonta ok?" I couldn't believe it, here we are both pouring out our feelings and he asks about my son. That made it even better to be back with him. No matter what the situation was he always thought about the kids. So I immediately said "YES" he's good I called him while you were inside.

Clifton told me that I had him under some type of spell because he had never spent this much money on a woman. Don't know how true that statement was but in a sense I believed him. Before I go on, let me just say that f I didn't mention this before I'll mention it now Clifton was very tight when it came to money and I truly mean "TIGHT" so I guess that's why he asked if I put some type of spell on him because he actually did spend some money. I took that as a complement and told him that it wasn't a spell it was just me and the woman that I am or maybe it was the fact that he knew what he wanted and knew just how to get her back.

That night was a beautiful night for us. Clifton never talked as much as he did that night. He told me everything and he again apologized several times. I was just glad to be back in his arms, in his presence, just with him period. The things he did that night is what kept me wanting him every single time I was near him. I would love to share what he did but a lot of it is too explicit to mention. I didn't want the night to end but it did but this time we both where we wanted to be and that was with each other.

A couple of months after Clifton and I got back together he had minor knee surgery. When it came to his health Clifton was very private and yes that really worked my nerve. When I had a small outpatient procedure he was there and was so helpful but when he had his knee surgery I didn't find out that he had surgery until I called him from work that evening and asked if he would ride somewhere with me and he responded that he couldn't because he had just had knee surgery, boy did that burn me up. After his surgery I called and went by his apartment every day after work making sure he was ok.

One particular day I called to let him know that I was on my way and asked if he needed anything. He said no at first but then stated that he did need his meds from Walgreens and asked if I would stay the night with him. He really didn't have to ask me that because that was my intention any way. So before I went to his place I stop to grab a couple of things from my place and made sure that Keyonta was okay because trust me I knew the drill. I called Clifton to inform him that I was on my way and asked if he was sure about not needing anything maybe even something to eat. He said no but there was something he wanted to eat at the house and that I could cook that for him.

    I thought that this man had learned from the first incident with me and other women but I guess he didn't. When I got to his place with my bag and his medicine in hand I rang his doorbell and to my surprise when I looked up at his window a young lady pulled back his shade. My blood pressure went from normal to boiling in 2.5 seconds. I was so tempted to drop his meds and buzz his bell again and say to him kiss my ASS!! But I didn't. I will tell you that I was madder than words could explain but for some strange reason something kept telling me it's okay, don't blow this out of proportion, clam down and take a deep breath. Clifton on crutches came down with the young lady. When he opened the door the young lady spoke to me and quickly got into her car. Clifton said quickly as well "sweetheart I work with her she's just one of my co-workers from the school and she was just dropping by to see how I was doing".

    With a blank but pist look on my face I didn't say a word, I nudged him to the side and walked or should I say stomped up the stairs. When we both got back into the apartment I threw his medicine at him and walked up to him and said " Clifton Lewis if you are lying to me I swear I am going to kick you in your damn knee, bust out your car windows and talk about you like a dog to everyone I know. I told you I will **NOT** go through this with you again and that's a promise".

Clifton promised me that I had nothing to worry about. He asked me to please trust him and that she was truly just a co-worker. Till this day I can say this: I don't know if she was actually a co-worker because I never met any of his co-workers from the grammar school where he worked part-time but I will say that after that encounter I don't know what he told her but I never saw her again.

Simple, But Truly Wonderful

Clifton loved to play basketball I think that's what brought him and my son so close to one another. Keyonta played high school basketball for Michele Clark and yes Clifton had his schedule for every game. When I could not make it to a game Keyonta would come home and say "Mom Cliff came to my game". You know that old saying "The way to a man's heart is to his stomach" well Clifton knew the way to mine. He knew that my son meant the world to me and the only other person that I would put before him was my Father GOD!

Clifton was so good with Keyonta. He came into Keyonta's life when he was 9 years old never disrespected or talked down to him. I found out that Clifton and Keyonta had conversation every other day. Keyonta said that he would call just to see how he was doing. Even when Clifton was on duty and he saw Keyonta out and about he would always stop him and ask was he ok and did he need anything. I can honestly say that Clifton was proud to tell people that although Keyonta was not his biological son he was his SON! And at no cost Keyonta was proud to call Clifton DAD! He actually called him pops which was hilarious because I thought it made Clifton feel old but Cliff didn't mind he actually liked it.

Every year Clifton made sure that he was at most of Keyonta regular season games and he made sure that he was at the Thanksgiving and Christmas tournaments too. It had gotten to the point where Keyonta's coaches and team mates would say "Keyonta now we see where you get your height from" and your Dad is a cool guy" Keyonta would laugh and say "yeah pops is a pretty cool dude".

When we were at the games I have to admit, there were times that Cliff thought he was the coach and the referee, he would nearly be on the court telling everybody what to do. Now could you imagine me 5'5 inches tall weighing about 160 trying to hold a 6'6 240 pound giant from going on the court and killing the referee's? Well that wasn't going to happen, so I had to remind him that it was ok to let the coaches and the ref's do their job and then maybe after the game he could speak to them to let them know what he thought about the teams playing but then again that wasn't a good idea either because I'd end up having the hardest time pulling "Mr. I should be the coach of the team myself" away when the games were over.

Now if you think that Clifton was bad at Keyonta's games you haven't heard anything yet! Cliff played on a league with a couple of his partners and friends. I didn't get a chance to go to all of those games, but the one's that I did have the opportunity to go to all I can say is I was glad when they won and was the first to want to leave when they lost. Cliff was a true team player but he hated to lose. No matter what the sport was if he was playing he was expecting a win no if's and's or buts' about it!

One particular basketball game that I attended with Cliff I sat in the stands with some of the other player's wives and or girlfriends and the first thing that one of them said to me was "girl your husband don't play when it comes to these games." Evidentially she must have seen him in rare form more than once. I laughed and asked "why do you say that? Her replay was Trice just wait and see. Oh GOD help me is what I was thinking.

As I sat and watched the game I saw what she was talking about. Clifton yelled and screamed at everybody even the referee's. Are you paying attention? What the hell were you thinking saying that? Refs are you woke? Pass the damn ball and stop being a ball hog and its called defense man damn! Was all I heard.

Trust me after that game and any other game that I would attend with him was over and they lost I would be scared to ride home with him. He talked about what they should have done, what they could have done and that it seemed that everybody on the team wasn't focused. I had to explain to him over and over again "Honey it's just a game, you win some and you loss some and plus you guys are not 16 years old anymore. You were playing against some guys that were in their early 20's who could run rings around you. Half of y'all were barely able to run up and down that darn court" but after a certain look he would give me (although he knew I was telling the truth) I would just say baby y'all got the next one don't worry about it.

Everyone had a story about Clifton and sports. One of his partners told me that he loved to play ball with Cliff because he knew just how to get under his skin; he knew it would piss him off even more if he teased him about the way he played. He told me that they were playing basketball one day and he blocked one of Cliff's shots. Afterwards he ran up on him and was like "yeah now what" he said Clifton hit him so hard in the chest and got all up in his face he literally had to remind him who he was. He said he told Cliff "hey big dog it's me and it's just a game". Eventually after the game was over (and yes they loss) Clifton apologized and asked was he ok.

    Period point blank my honey didn't take well to losing, as I said he expected to win all the time. I knew all about competiveness, winning and losing, but all in fun. So trying to rub that off on Clifton was a huge challenge. Like I said everyone had a sports tale about Clifton and all I can say is that they were all the same so with a very sincere apology let me say that I am so sorry for the sports monster that you all had to put up with.

Wanting Him to Love Living

My family loved Clifton and he loved them back as well. I will admit he wasn't too crazy about everybody but they would never know it, and sorry family but I'm not telling either. Cliff had his favorite aunts and cousin, but if you ask my Aunt Pier she would tell you "I AM HIS FAVORITE AUNT AND DON'T YOU FOR GET IT! Pier and Clifton were at each other throats every time they were around one another. They were words with friend's buddies and let me tell you it was never pretty with those two. There were countless times were Cliff "accused" Pier of cheating and using a dictionary because he never understood how she was able to come up with the words that she did. As always Pier would throw it in his face "No Cliff I don't use a dictionary I am just that smart and you are just a sore loser!" I would always be placed right in the middle of their little words with friend's war.

I would just sit and listen and say "that's why I don't play that game and I have nothing to do with it so please leave me out of y'all mess!"

I can even recall one night at about 1:30 in the morning, Clifton and I were in bed and I see him on his phone, I say to him "baby why you are on the phone at 1:30 in the morning"? Mind you he had just got off of work at 12:30am so you would think that the only thing that would be on his mind was going to sleep. **NO!** He told me that he had to find a word that would give him the win and I said a word, a win? Are you playing words with friends with Pier at this time of morning? He said "yeah and if I place this last word I am going to win this game".

I could not believe what I was hearing; basically I was so out done. Of course when he placed that word and it gave him the win he screamed out "YES I BEAT HER!! At 1:30 in the morning and then he texted her and said "who's the sore loser now". This battle went on for years, oh and let me just say that yes Pier thought that she won that game and when she finally found out that he actually did win she simply text him back "WHATEVER CLIFF YOU ARE STILL A SORE LOSER"

  Clifton and I traveled a lot with my family but we also made it appoint to travel alone or with just our little family the kids (Keyonta and Simone). One year we all went as a family to The Mall of America in Minnesota. Now before I go any further I must let you know that I come from a very large family and Clifton always said "I really have to get use to this". (Having so many family members around all the time) Anyway as were driving down Clifton told me two things, (1) "Sweetheart remember we will need some place to sit so don't go buying the entire mall, and (2) "give me your checkbook" he literally took my checkbook from me.

  When we got to the hotel of course we were the last one's to get there my Uncle Lamar and Aunt Pier teased us about it, "He comes Cliff and Latrice 5 hours late" and my honey's response to that was "in your words Pier WHATEVER" . After we were settled in we all went and did a little shopping I was so glad that Keyonta and Michael had their own hotel room because some of the things that I bought that Clifton didn't know about was held in their room and because I am loved by both boys so much Clifton never knew a thing!

What I found hilariously funny was that Cliff told me not to go overboard shopping but he literally had more bags than I did, but of course he debated that. When we got back to the hotel Clifton said to me "Sweetheart do you really need everything you bought"? Of course being a woman if I bought it, it needed it, but what he didn't know was that some of the things that were in my bags were for him, Keyonta, Simone, and our mothers. "Sweetheart I bet you bought something for everybody in your family and I bet you bought something for the kids who don't need a thing" which was his favorite thing to say. But I too had a favorite saying "Honey it was on sale"!

Cliff had a really good time while we were in Minnesota because Clifton said that we would do Mall Of America every year sometimes with the kids and the family and then other times it would be just us he and I but I would be placed on a strict budget. Really, I know Clifton knew me better than that.

He knew for a fact that I would find a way around that budget stuff because a real shopaholic always does, but I also knew that I didn't want to push Clifton. I believed him when he said that he would take my check book and stuff because he'd done it before and he knew that taking my check book and credit cards away was like taking all the breath that I had in my body. I would be lifeless so whatever I was going to do it would have to be something that papa Lewis would never in a million years get wind of. For the record Clifton was a great provider, I never wanted or needed for anything. He was the one who actually taught me how to be a more conservative spender but I won't lie I have slipped several times and to this day I still do.

One year I won a trip to New Orleans. Without any hesitation I called Cliff and told him "Baby pack your bags we are on our way to New Orleans for the Essence Music Festival". He said "you are lying" and I said to him "fine I'll just find someone else to take". After he thought about it he asked me how we were going to New Orleans. I told him thanks to quick hand dialing and WGCI we are on our way!!! That was a beautiful way for Clifton and I to really wrap ourselves in one another. We had time to talk about the present and also our future. It also gave us a chance to witness New Orleans being re-built after hurricane Katrina.

While in New Orleans Clifton told me for the first time that he thinks he's actually falling for me. I didn't know how to take that because we had been dating for a while now so I thought the "falling for me" part was already taken care of, but I guess it wasn't. I will say he couldn't have chosen a better place to tell me, on vacation, in his arms, in New Orleans. He said that his feelings for me were growing stronger and stronger, and I don't know why, but again he said that I had placed some type of voodoo on him. He said "it must be some type of spell because I said that I wasn't going to devote myself, giving my all to another woman again. But in comes "Ms. Tucker" who is very demanding, spoiled and who doesn't take no for an answer got me feeling a little different. You actually got me thinking a few things, but right now you don't need to know what they are".

I was flattered and overjoyed because Clifton's brick wall was starting to crack. But there were still times where I thought I took two bricks out but somehow he'd put 4 bricks back in. Didn't matter, I thanked God for giving me the insight and the ways to make Mr. Lewis realize that it was all about what he had in the inside that made my attraction for him and to him worth all the fight that he was giving me. Of course he had me wondering and thinking and wanting to know what his thoughts were but as long as I had him thinking it really didn't matter, hopefully the things that he was thinking were good.

I told Cliff over and over again that we both had relationships that we were not too proud of but we couldn't let that rock the foundation what we were trying to build on. I never compared him to anyone one that I had dated in the past so I wanted him to do the same for me. He agreed but he still was "a little cautious" but it seemed like I was finally getting that "Great wall of Clifton" torn down.

After our return from New Orleans Cliff went back to doing what he did best WORKING!!! This man worked so much that it made me sick. I always said that he didn't get the proper rest, he didn't eat right but that didn't stop him. He was determined to make sure that his family was taken care of.

He would always tell me "Trice I have to get this for Simone or I have to do this for Simone which was never a problem. I loved the fact that he loved his daughter and would go above and beyond for her I never saw anything different. As a matter of fact he never forgot to include Keyonta. If Keyonta called and said he needed whatever, Cliff was "Johnny on the spot" period point blank "his" kids had what they needed.   He wasn't into giving the kids everything they wanted but he gave them what they needed. I remember when Simone asked him to get her a laptop. He said that she was too young to have a lap top and that she would get one when he felt that she was responsible enough and old enough to have one.

He wasn't too happy about her having a cell phone either but I had to let him know that I disagreed and I think that she should have a cell phone; it's too much happening for her not to have a phone. Anything could happen and she needed to be able to contact someone in case of an emergency. He agreed but we never talked about it again because eventually Simone's mother got her a phone against his wishes but I thought it was for the best.

Clifton worked as a part-time security guard for Wal-Mart was I happy about that no, and I wasn't happy about the fact that he also worked other little side jobs when he could. I got so fed up with him working so much that I purposely planned a trip to California. I booked the flights, our hotel and gave Clifton the dates. I told him that I could not get my money back so he would have to do some magic and work on getting some days off. He was so mad at me but I didn't care. I wanted him to relax and start enjoying life, I wanted to take work off of his mind for a while, hell he needed some stress free days.

We had wonderful time while we were there. My stepdad resides in California so we were able to visit him and I also met a very close friend of Cliff's. Our trip was adventurous, amusing and eventful. We both packed for "hot weather" and it rained 3 days while we were there but that was fine because we were able to relax in our hotel room and relaxed is really what Clifton did. He slept half the days away which didn't bother me because that's what I wanted him to do but I also wanted him to enjoy himself as well. Of course my enjoyment came when Clifton told me that we were going to the mall but we were only going because we were meeting his friend there. That didn't matter to me because I was excited about that fact that I was in a shopping mall; but my baby wasn't having it. He told me very sternly "sweetheart no shopping". Oh I could have died right there but I was glad that he was so stern because I knew that I wouldn't have been able to control myself. Plus he said that I couldn't use his suit case to put anything "extra" in.

While vacationing in California he craziest thing happened. We were in our hotel's parking lot coming in from dinner with my step-dad when this guy comes from out of nowhere and approach's Cliff. The funny part of this was that the guy was like 4 feet nothing compared to Clifton. The guy looked Clifton up and down and said "A is yo name Kevin nigga" Clifton looked at the guy like he had a problem and said "No my name is not Kevin." Mind you I opened the car door getting ready to get out and Clifton said "Sweetheart stay in the car" and I said "No" and I got out. The guy was still standing there rocking side to side he stopped and asked Clifton again "Is your name Kevin"? Clifton said "Look man I told you my name is not Kevin what the hell is your problem".

The guy asked Clifton was his woman in there. At this point I walked around to where Clifton and this guy was standing and I said to Clifton "Baby let's just walk away from him, he must be high or something". Believe it or not this guy was still talking crazy and started to walk up on Clifton. Yes I started to panic and thought I do not want to go to jail in California for murder because that is what was about to happen. Clifton told that guy "Look man if I tell you one more time that my name is not Kevin and if you keep walking up on me I am going to knock the shit out of you so back the fuck up"! Clifton balled up his hand but at that moment one of the staff members came out to the parking lot and asked if we were ok.

      We explained to him that this guy was harassing us. The hotel attendant told the guy to go about his business, the guy then said to the attendant "What you want some of this too". The attendant said again to the guy, look you need to leave. The guy then turned to Cliff and said "Nigga you sure yo name ain't Kevin" Clifton moved towards the guy but I grabbed him by the arm and said "baby no let the hotel personnel handle this". I understood why Clifton was trying to help the hotel attendant, he wasn't any taller than that crazy ass man and he really didn't speak English to well either. The hotel attendant finally got the guy to leave the parking lot and Clifton and I headed back into the hotel. As we were getting on the elevator we warned this other couple about that guy and told them to be careful as they were heading out. When we finally got into our hotel room I looked at Clifton and said "Mr. CPD we almost needed the LAPD, what a welcome to Cali we got". We both laughed then he said to me "Trice next time I tell you to stay in the car and you get out I am going to kick your butt" and I told him "no you're not because no matter what situation we're in, we are in it together we'll both go out fighting" and he said "Yeah okay after I shoot the person I am going to kill you for being so damn hard headed" he then kissed me and said I am about to hit the shower you coming? Oh how I love this man.

The next day after our night of "boys in the hood" we had the chance to enjoy a day at universal studios. They had this booth where you put this suit on and it's like there is no gravity so you literally float into the air. Clifton wanted to try it out so bad, but sad to say he was too "big" for the suit so that was that. We had signs made. Clifton's sign said "DON'T BE AFRAID OF THE DOGS, BE AFRAID OF THE OWENER" I had one made for Keyonta that said KEYONTA'S ROOM and we also had one made for Simone that said PRINCESS SIMONE'S ROOM. After we had our signs made we had dinner with Clifton's friend. He said to me "You must be really special to my boy here because you are the first person to get him to come to California; I've been trying to get him to come out here for years. All I can say is welcome to the family". Thank you I said and yes I will admit I patted myself on the shoulder because yes I DID THAT.

His friend then asked that infamous question that Clifton dreaded "So when are you guys going to tie the knot" Clifton response to that was "Man not you too" Cliff hated that question almost as bad as people always asking us "when are you two going to have a baby". I won't lie to you I hated that baby question too. After me acting like I wasn't interested in what Clifton and his friend were talking about I asked his friends girlfriend the same question and she said yes they are going to get married but I can't recall if she said they were getting married in a couple of months or the following year. I do recall me looking at Clifton and saying "babe we'll be coming back to Cali for a wedding won't we; and under my breath I said I'll be glad when I'll be able to invite people to my wedding" Clifton looked at me and said "No doubt" wouldn't miss my boy's wedding for nothing" then he said "sweetheart did you say something else"? The look on my face probably gave me away, but I said to him "NO you must be hearing things" (God he had very good hearing).

We really had a good time in California. We returned on Sunday and yes Clifton was back to work that Monday. Who does that? Usually you would need a day to settle down after coming back from vacation (at least I do) but not Mr. Lewis he was back on the grind first thing Monday morning. I know that he had a good time but I always had this inkling in the back of my mind that Clifton was thinking about work all while we were on vacation.

What Cliff didn't know was that I agreed for us to go to the circle city classic in Indianapolis with some of my family members. I was thinking really hard, trying to figure out how I was going to tell him this one. Oh I prayed and told him one night over dinner. "Baby did I tell you that we were going to the Circle City Classic with Pier and Lamar, Lori and Courtney and a couple other people". He looked at me and said "since when?" I tried to say all in one breath "Since Pier asked if we wanted to go and I said yes and paid for our tickets and booked our hotel room because we're staying the weekend". Well that one breath thing didn't work and the expression on Clifton face was one that I will never forget.

He stopped chewing his food and stood up and turned towards me. I didn't know if I should run or start crying right where I was sitting, I just knew that I was done for. Clifton said "Why would you do something like that without consulting with me first" but he said it calmly which really scared me because I know that he was mad as hell but he didn't raise his voice not one time. I told him that I didn't think he would mind, plus it was the weekend that he was off. He said "how do you know I'm off that weekend" I said "because I asked you and you said yeah why" Clifton then turned so red in the face and that's when I got up from the table and proceed to walk towards any open door. He said "Ms. Tucker you think you know everything. Yeah I am off that weekend but I was planning to work my part-time.

You're always doing something without asking and let me guess you can't get your money back". I had to let him calm down a little. Later on that evening I apologized and told him that if he didn't want to go I would cancel the hotel reservations and I could sell our tickets. He looked at me with his I don't believe you face and said "no it's all good because I know you want to go, you always want to go". Then he said "Listen it would be cool if you ask me or let me know in advance that you are making plans for us to do something. Tamara we don't always have to do stuff just because somebody else is doing it, it's alright to stay at home sometimes. (This in translation meant we don't have to spend money). God I hated when he was right but everything I did or wanted to do I wanted him with me no matter what it was.

I knew for a fact that Clifton loved to be at home and so did I but I wanted him to live a little I wanted him to get away from the "ESPN" network. When his partners would call and ask him to hang out for awhile Clifton usually turned them down. He always had some strange reason as to why he didn't want to go and I was one of them, well that's what I was told any way. I think he only told me that to make me feel good and it did so I didn't mind being his excuse sometimes.

When Clifton did go out he didn't stay long. He would leave at around 8:00pm and would be back home before or around 11:00pm. I would say to him "baby what are you doing back so soon?" And he would say "no reason I was just ready to come home". I would beg for him to stay out later than 11:00, I would even help him get dressed. I would pick out the freshest fit, and made sure he was cleaned shaved. Hell he would look so good that I would have to control myself and you all know what I mean.

It was the same way when we were in Indianapolis. That was one of wildest and side hurting from laughter weekends we spent together.

We were in downtown Indianapolis looking for a good spot to eat, we found this place that sold chicken and waffles. I don't recall the actual name of the restaurant but they did serve good food. After dinner we all went back to the hotel and being that I am a student at De Paul University I chose to shower and grab my laptop and books to study everyone else went in changed clothes and was heading out for awhile. I had to get a paper done before the weekend was over so I couldn't go but I told Clifton that he should go. He procrastinated a while until he found out they were going to a strip club.

He got all cleaned up and then sat next to me and said "Sweetheart are you sure you are ok with me going out with them without you"? I said to him YES! Go and have a good time you deserve it, plus I have to get this paper done so I can't go. He asked again "are you sure"? I literally got up helped him finish getting himself together and then took him by the hand and opened the door and said "kiss me" he did and I pushed him out the door and said have a good time stay out as late as you want to and I closed the door behind him.

I don't know what time he actually got back to the hotel but when he came into the room I looked at the clock and it said 3:30 am. I said to him "I am so proud of you" and the first thing he said was "Baby don't believe nothing Pier and the rest of them tell you". Then he went on to say that Pier and Lamar are something else. I asked "why do you say that"? He said just listen. As I sat up in the bed I heard my aunt and her hubby arguing so I asked Clifton what was that all about? As he began to tell me what happen I laughed and said" yeah you are right only those two".

The morning of the game we all went to breakfast. Clifton asked Lamar was everything ok and my Uncle Lamar being his usually self and said "Yeah man you know how the wife is but hey I love her". Of course Pier over heard the conversation between Clifton and Lamar and said "Cliff I know you are not talking. Did you tell Trice how that stripper took your glasses off your face and gave you lap dance"? I turned and looked at Clifton and said "REALLY" you forgot to tell me that part last night. So she took your glasses off your face and gave you lap dance? At his defense was my Uncle Lamar, my cousin Toccara's friend Rock , and my cousin Lori's husband Courtney. "It wasn't like he was there by himself we were all sitting at the table and she did not give him a private lap dance, she danced for all of us". Again I looked at Cliff and said "You let some other female take your glasses off your face and then dance in front of you half naked and on top of that you willingly gave money? Oh my God if you could have seen the expression on Clifton's face it was **PRICELESS!!** I tried really hard not to laugh directly at him but I was boiling over with laughter in the inside due to the fact that he was speechless. Guess the cat really had his tongue that time.

Of course I was enjoying every bit of the torcher that Clifton was being put through. So I continued on with it a little while longer. "I can't believe that some other female touched my man glasses. As a matter of fact the glasses that I love to see him in because they make me wanted to jump his bones in an instant, then he turns around and gives her money that he claimed he didn't have when I asked if I could get that pair of boots yesterday. Oh baby you got a lot of explaining to do when we get back to our room".

Still trying to act like I was upset about what I just heard I walked away from Cliff but I only did that because I had to laugh but again I couldn't do it in his face. Cliff looked at Pier, Toccara and my other cousin Lori and said "WHATEVER" and then asked Pier "Why are you always trying to start something? I can't help it because you got mad that Lamar got a lap dance too and wasn't paying any attention to you". From there the fight was on but of course it was a loving fight no one was harmed.

After a good laugh I finally had to admit to Clifton that I was only playing and I didn't care that the stripper took off his glasses and I am glad that he had a good time. But I also told him that if I ever find out that someone else is giving him a lap dance and places his glasses in places that they have no busy being, he will have a problem for real and her name is ME so he'd better arrange for the CPD to have my cell ready! Clifton went on to say "Sweetheart the next time we go anywhere with Pier and Lamar I am going to make sure that Lamar chains Pier up so she can't get out of their hotel room. That damn girl starts too much trouble". All in all, that trip turned out to be one of the best trips we had taken outside of our other travels and with some of my family.

Although Clifton hated to take off from work each time we returned from a mini-vacation he would always say "Baby thanks I needed that" and my reply would always be "yes you did can't wait until we do it again."

Still Moving Forward

The best thing about our relationship was that fact that we didn't argue. We disagreed a lot but our disagreements didn't turn into world war two. I think that had a lot to do with fact that Clifton was a Taurus and I am a Libra and if things didn't balance out for me something would be done where things became balanced. Cliff on the other hand was very stubborn and set in his ways. It was his way or no way at all, no matter what it was he had a rational explanation for everything.

I never wanted to be apart from him and I know (well I hoped) that he felt the same way although he would never in a million years admit that. Before we decided to live together we would take turns staying at each other's apartments. I never wanted him to go back to his place but he always had two good reasons as to why he could not stay longer than a night or two at my place with me and two was actually pushing it. Fat boy one of his pit bulls and Fiona that darn cat were his two reasons. At first and yes I will admit that I was a little jealous of the animals because sometimes I felt like they were getting a lot of his attention and I didn't want to share him with anyone except for his daughter and his mom but I came to realize that I had to compromise and not be so selfish.

I recall one night he went to pick his daughter up. At that time he was still living in his apartment. He called me as they were heading back from the movies and said to me "Hey I would like for you to go out to grab a bite to eat with us" of course I said yes so he picked me up and we went to dinner. That was a very nice dinner date because I really didn't get the chance to see Simone that often because of her dad's work schedule. Keyonta didn't go to dinner with us because he spent the night at his friend Ronnie's house. Any way after dinner to my surprise Simone asked her dad "Daddy is Trice coming back to your house with us"? Clifton and I looked at each other and he said "sure she can if she wants to", and I said if she wants me to come then I am there.

We laughed and talk for a while longer and after dinner we went back to Cliff's apartment. I helped Simone get her bath and we sat and watched TV together until she fell asleep. Clifton said to me "Sweetheart hope you don't mind sleeping on the edge of the bed because she's a wilder sleeper "and I said to him "Why don't we let her have the bed and we take the floor in the living room" he said "the floor, you want us to sleep on the floor"? And I said yes why not it's carpeted? He gave me a kiss on the cheek and said I guess and yes I know I have carpet but if my back starts to hurt I am leaving you on that hard carpeted floor and I am going to get in my softly padded bed. Little did he know that if he had of gotten up to get in the bed I was heading straight for the couch.

At about 2:00 in the morning I awoke and saw that Simone had gotten out of bed and laid on the couch. I put a blanket over her but as I did her dad awoke and said "sweetheart why didn't you tell me she was lying there"? I told him that it was fine but he said no it's not. He picked her up and took her back into the bedroom. Simone was half awake and half sleep when she said to her daddy "why can't I sleep in here with you"? He didn't give her a reason why he just said because you can't and carried her back into the bedroom. I wanted to say something so bad but I left it alone. I never said anything to him when it came to his decisions about his daughter and he gave me the same respect when it came to my son, but we did let one another voice our opinions.

He always felt that sometimes I was too easy on the kids, but underneath that big frame of his he was just as soft as I was. Keyonta was 17 years old and Clifton would still ask me have I talked to Keyonta if he wasn't home at a certain time. As a matter of fact one night we were on our way to do laundry, Keyonta wasn't home and once we got everything inside the car Clifton asked "Trice where's Keyonta? I said I don't know but he did say that he was stopping by his friend's house for a while. Clifton's reply was "What friend and where does this friend live? "Baby his friend lives on Augusta and Laramie somewhere I don't know exactly where". Why did I say that, Clifton jumped into "police/dad" mode. "What do you mean you don't know exactly where? Call him and ask where this friend lives.   It is too much going on out in these streets for us not to know where he is" (Oh now my words were being thrown back in my face). Nothing I said could calm him down, so I called Keyonta and said "Keyonta please tell Cliff where you before he kills me".   Keyonta told me that he was on Laramie and Augusta and to tell "pops" that he was ok. I relayed the message to Clifton but he was still in his police/dad mode and said yeah okay but where is he on Laramie and Augusta?

    I went back and forth with Keyonta until he said "mom tell Cliff I am right up the street from the house". We drove until we saw Keyonta.   Thank God that he was actually standing outside of his friend's house because as we pulled up Clifton let down the window like we were casing the house or something. I just sled down in the seat and shook my head. Keyonta laughed and said to Clifton "pops I told my mom that I was cool".   Clifton said "She told me". I then sat up in the seat and said "Yeah I did tell him what you said but Mr. Over protective had to see for himself". "How long will you be here"? Cliff asked.   Keyonta's response was "pops I 'm not sure but I'll be okay. Clifton said "Well just make sure that you call us when you get to the house. This was his position all the time. This 6 foot 6 inch person who could intimidate or even better put the fear of God in anyone never did. He was always this soft and warm person with a positive mind and an even bigger heart but if you made him mad let's just say I would hate to be you.

It was very rare that Clifton was seen angry or upset. If you ever wanted to see Clifton in rare form you would have had to either go to one of his basketball games or come over to the house when either the bears or the bulls where playing. I would do nothing but sit back and watch. You would have thought that we were either at the United Center or in Solider Field itself. He would literally curse at the television throw things and call the plays and all I would say is "Baby we are at home, the refs can't hear you we are watching the game on TV we are not there, so please clam down" and I would get this look as if I have sinned against God himself. Sometimes it got so bad that I would make up a reason to leave and I would come back once I thought the game was over.

As the years passed everything just felt right for Clifton and I. We embraced each other more and more. Clifton was my protector, my lover, and most important my best friend. He was the person I turned to before I would go to anyone else; so I knew I had no worries.   We started making plans to make our family complete. Now for the record we never EVER talked about having more children because we were content with the two that we had. We talked more and more about what our future held, what we wanted for our kids and for ourselves. College for the kids and plenty of vacationing for us (the kids would be included sometimes).

I remember the day he got a phone call from his mom informing him that his aunt had passed away. I had never seen him cry and at that moment our roles reversed. I felt like his protector, I just held him and told him that everything was going to be okay. That really took a toll on him because the day his aunt passed was actually his brother Michael's birthday so that was like a double heart breaker for him but I never left his side. I let him cry and held him as he did. Yes it was hard for me to see him like that but I am so glad I did because that showed me that he knew how to cry and what it felt like to hurt. This also became my opportunity to let him know that I was there and forever will be and that it was okay to let me carry the weight sometimes. Meaning that he could put his pride aside and not always be the "strong one" all the time.

In that same year (2010) my heart was torn out of my chest. We were planning a trip to Wisconsin Dells everyone was so excited especially me because I finally had all of my brothers with me and it was a huge family trip. I was at home cooking dinner and my brother James came by because he was informed that I was cooking Mac and cheese which was his favorite. James and I had a very long big sister/ little brother talk. He told me that he was happy that I have finally found somebody that makes me smile and someone that made him wear his seat belt even though he didn't want to. We talked about him being in my wedding which my brother said "would be soon" I guess he knew something that I didn't but I was glad to hear it.

After James was done eating I asked him if he could take me to the station so I could get the car from Clifton. He did and made me laugh all the way there because he had that darn seat belt on and was driving with both hands on the wheel. I Asked James was he ok and he said "yeah tudda (my nick name that my brothers call me) I am good I just can't believe I am going to the police station on my own free will" I laughed and told him that he would be okay.

I called Cliff to inform him that I was outside of the station. He came out all in dressed in uniform and my brother got out the car and said "Bro, you make me feel safe in these streets, I see ya banger and stuff you all good" Cliff smiled and said "Cut that out" They chatted for a minute before Clifton gave me the keys to the car. My brother said to him "Bro are you ready for this weekend? Cliff responded "Yeah I'm ready you know your sister made sure of that". "Yeah I know how tudda can be but that's alright we'll get her butt this weekend because you know she can't swim". After hearing all of that I look and the both of them and said "look I don't play in water so the both of y'all better leave me alone". They both laughed. Clifton gave me the keys to the car and James got back into his car but before he pulled off he said "tudda are you good? I told him yeah I'm good and I asked him was he good and he said "yeah I am all good, my sister fed me and my bro is protecting me what more can I ask for. I am about to go to the crib and relax".

6 hours later my cell phone kept ringing and I was like "who keeps calling me at this time of night" so I decided to check my voice mail and the message that I got nearly took all the breath out of my body. The message said "Trice you need to get here right away James just got shot, they shot James" I dropped my phone; my mind was racing my chest hurting and tears falling. I got in the car and ran every red light and stop sign. I didn't care about anything or anyone else; I had to get to my brother. When I got to where my brother was there were police cars and tape everywhere I saw my family member running and

crying. I remember jumping over the police tape and screaming where is he? Where's my brother?

People were grabbing me saying "No Trice you don't want to see him like that" I wasn't trying to hear what they were talking about, I just wanted my brother. Still people were trying to hold me back until I found myself on the ground next thing I know I was being picked up off the ground by Clifton he grabbed me and told me to pull myself together he said "Baby I am going to take care of this I promise." He carried me into my grandmother's house and sat me on the couch and said "sweetheart I promise we will take care of this" stop crying.

I held on to his words. Clifton was there with me every step of the way. He hated going to hospitals but when they called me and told me that there was nothing more that they could do for my brother he held my hand and went to the hospital with me. I lost my brother on August 9th 2010.

My world caved in on me, but Clifton always found a way to dig me out, he always knew the right words to say. He kept me encouraged and inspired me to never forget that my brother will always be with me. It was Clifton's decision to keep our plans of going to Wisconsin. He said I needed or should I say we needed something to take our minds of our loss. I was a bit shocked because I figure this was a good reason for him **not** to have to take off from work but as I stated Clifton never let me hurt, he always tried to keep a smile on my face during my (our) time of bereavement. He knew what I was going through because he had already been through it some years earlier with his brother.

That weekend was one of many that I never wanted to end. That Saturday evening the kids were at the pool, Clifton and I were in the room trying to figure out what restaurant we were going to for dinner. As I sat on the balcony of our hotel room tears began to stream down my face. All I could think of was my brother James and how he was suppose to be there with me. Cliff came out onto the balcony with me and pulled me into his arms and said to me "Sweetheart everything will be okay, JB (James) wouldn't want you out here like this. I know it's hard but we will get through this together. I know how much you loved your brother and you know how much your brother loved you so you've got to pull it together".

I just laid upon his chest and thanked him for being there. Of course I had to look up to him and as he looked down at me he said "Ms. Tucker (with a little hesitation) when we get back to Chicago I want you to contact your landlord and let her know that you'll be moving in a couple of months". In disbelief I said "what"? He said "you heard me, with Keyonta getting ready to go off to school I don't want you over at that apartment by yourself so once we get back home you need to start making arrangements.

I must admit I was taken for a loop because I wasn't expecting that to come out of his mouth. The first thing that came to my mind was the day he took me over to the house and he said to me "what do you think about **MY HOUSE?** And when I corrected him saying "You mean what do I think about **OUR** house" he didn't comment he just said yeah yeah whatever. Was this something that he had already been thinking about before all of this happened? It's crazy because when I talked about us moving in together he blew it off or always changed the subject and now out of nowhere I'm making arrangements to move. Life as I knew it was changing and it was a change that I had been waiting on for a long time. Without hesitation I said to Clifton "Are you serious"? He looked and me and said "Yeah I am". I don't know what brought this on. I don't know if it was because I had just experienced the tragic loss of my brother or maybe I had finally gotten to the depth of "Mr. Lewis heart". No matter what it was I was getting what I wanted finally and it only took me 8 ½ years to get it. Getting what I wanted didn't refer to the fact that Clifton asked me to move in with him, it referred to the fact that Cliff finally let me take the last brick out of the wall that was so hard to tear down at first.

We finished our weekend in Wisconsin and came back to Chicago to lay my brother to rest. I don't know which was worst watching my family, my mother and brothers struggle with our loss or watching Clifton trying to hold his word and be there for me and reliving the fact that he had just lost another "brother" as well.

Reality, As Real As It Can Get

2010 became the year of Clifton, Latrice and our family. Clifton's mom told me that he always said that he only wanted one child and I was fine with that because I felt the same way. But one day when Cliff and I where home he said to me "sweetheart you know Keyonta is a good kid, you're doing an excellent job with him". I said "thanks but don't forget that you have been in his life since he was 9 so you've played a part in that too". He smiled and said "I remember when I said that I only wanted one child, but God saw fit for me to have two my son and my daughter". When he said those words to me I felt chills all over my body. Everything fell into place for me at last. As a mother my main concern was that I would find someone that my son would be okay with. But what was even more important to me was that someone be okay with my son. I am more than pleased to say that I found that someone and his name was Clifton P. Lewis.

As we were transitioning into making two homes one I had to constantly explain to Cliff that he would have to adjust to a few things and the same would go for me and my son. As Clifton knew my son had a few close friends but his best friend more like his brother was Ronnie. Ronnie and Keyonta have been friends since 2nd grade and where you saw one you were sure to see the other. It was hard for me to tell Ronnie that we are staying at the house now and that sometimes he couldn't stay. So a month before we moved everything out of the apartment I would let the boys camp out there every now and then.

One night Clifton told me that his (our) nephew Michael was coming over and yes every time Mike came over they all hung out together. This particular time that Mike was over all the boys were upstairs (their usual spot) playing the game. I noticed that we were out of a few things so I informed Cliff that I was running out to store. On my way out Michael asked if he could ride with me of course I said yes, mind you Ronnie and Keyonta were still up stairs.

Mike and I went to target and on our way back he asked me was Ronnie going to stay with us tonight? I told him that I didn't care but we had to ask his uncle. Michael called Clifton and said "Uncle Cliff I was calling to ask you if it was okay for Ronnie to stay over with me and Keyonta tonight"? The first thing that came out of Cliff's mouth was "Trice put you up to this didn't she"? Mike said "No she didn't" I asked her if Ronnie could stay over with us and she told me that I would have to ask you. You could hear Clifton screaming in the background saying "yeah right she didn't". My God the fight was on once Michael and I got back to the house. I couldn't even get my coat off before "BIG" papa Lewis came out of the bedroom into the kitchen ranting.

Michael went back up stairs and words began to fly. "Trice you made Michael call me and ask if Ronnie could stay didn't you?" "No I didn't, he asked me if he could say over with him and Keyonta and I told him that I didn't care but he would have to ask you, so if you feel like that's me putting him up to asking you then yes, yes I did" Clifton began to walk towards me and I politely started to walk the other way (which was actually around the kitchen table) He had this look like he wanted to choke the life out of me. I wanted to laugh but I couldn't because I knew he was serious. "Tamara he said (he only calls me Tamara when he is mad with me) where is he suppose to sleep?" I looked at him and said "Really Cliff, they are boys they don't care about sleeping arrangements. As long as they have that Xbox, their cell phones and their lap tops they are good, again they are boys they'll put blankets on the floor. He just looked at me, but then I thought about it "Wait, did you forget that we bought two queen size air mattresses?"

Cliff stormed out of the kitchen saying "I don't know why you are trying to make me look like the fucking bad guy. If I say no then they'll be upset with me" then he slammed the bedroom door in my face as I was approaching it. The boys all ran down the stairs and asked me was everything ok? I told all of them including Michael to gather up their things because we were going to stay the night at the apartment and I would call them when I was ready to leave. Keyonta looked at me and said "Ma are you sure everything is alright"? I told him yes and they all went back upstairs.

Once the boys were back up stairs I pushed the bedroom door open. Clifton was sitting at the foot of the bed looking at his phone I walked in and stood directly in front of him and said "If you ever slam another door in my face that will be the last damn door you slam on anybody. Ain't nobody trying to make you look like anything, right now you are making yourself look like the fucking bad guy. Why would the boys be upset with you if you said no? Hell this is your house and if you say no then it is what it is NO! As a matter of fact I'm not even staying here tonight I am taking the boys Michael included and we are going back to the apartment". I had never talked to Clifton like that but I was so mad and I didn't care, whatever came out just came out. I told him that I didn't have to put up with his nasty attitude and that he should take that out on whoever it was that pisted him off because it wasn't me nor the boys. I walked out of the bedroom and called for the boys to come down.

They all came down with their back packs and as we were heading to the door Clifton came out of the room stood in front of the door and said " Keyonta y'all can gone back upstairs, and Ronnie it's cool you can stay." At this point the boys turned around and looked at me. He said to them "No need to look at her she has nothing to say". I was just dumb founded. Not even 15 minutes ago this big angry man was about to tear the hinges of the bedroom door, cursing and fusing then all of a sudden his whole damn demeanor changes and know he's as calm as his damn cat. Keyonta looked at me and said "Ma so are we staying or not"? For a moment I was speechless, I could do nothing but look at Clifton.

I then turned to Keyonta and said "You know son I am confused, I don't know. Then I turned to Cliff and said "Are we staying?" He told the boys to gone back up stairs and finish playing the game or whatever they were doing. He also told them that we were going to order a pizza or something later. The boys went back up stairs. I just stood at the back door coat still on and hand still on the door knob. Clifton walked up to me and said "Ms Tucker you can take your hand off the door knob and take that darn coat off I know you're hot."

If only he knew what was going through my head at that moment, trust and believe it was nothing nice. I think I stood by the door for a good 5 minutes because I could not believe what just happened. I finally took my coat off laid it across the kitchen chair and walked into the living room. I sat quietly on the couch didn't turn on the television, lights, nothing. I literally sat in the dark. Tears started to run down my face for two reasons: (1) I didn't understand why things blew up the way they did and (2) I don't know how many times I told Clifton that I hated to argue. Clifton came into living room where I was sat next to me and wiped my face and said to me "Sweetheart don't cry I'm sorry I lost my head for a minute, I apologize".

I looked at him and said "Cliff what the hell were we arguing about? I only told Michael to ask you because I respect you and our home. Baby you have more say so then I do. I told you once before that Ronnie staying over every now and then was one of the things that you would have to get used to, and I was not about to tell Ronnie that he had to go home after he's been with Keyonta and Mike all day. He said to me "I know sweetheart you're right. I didn't mean to blow up like that and yes I did forget about the air mattresses up there. I'm so sorry now stop crying". I told him that I never wanted to argue like that again and he said to me "I promise we won't".

Clifton was a man of his word. We never argued again but as I stated earlier we did disagree on several occasions especially when it came to certain things like the kids, the house and shopping. Oh my God especially shopping. I never knew why Cliff would even bother going through a shopping dispute with me. Shopping is my past time and I do it very well. And I did it or should I say I do it without "breaking the bank" especially the first bank of Clifton Lewis. It was rule of thumb that we never kept track of each other money but we always made sure the bills were paid before anything else.

I remember when we went to get furniture for the house on our way Clifton gave me this huge speech about the amount he plan to spend and that I was only to give my opinion. He knew that with me price was never an issue. If I saw something I liked no matter what the price was, I bought it. So I don't know what he meant when he said I could only give my opinion; but I knew I was going to do more than that. I had already envisioned what would go nice in each room. I was going for color scheme, something that we both liked and agreed on, and also something that would leave a good impression on our guest whenever we would have company over. The funny part about all of that was when I said "company" he looked at me and said, "Don't worry about company we won't be inviting people over less is best". Again that went into to one ear and out of the other.

While in the furniture store we looked around for a while, I waited patiently for Clifton to ask me what I thought about a few of the pieces that he picked. I can honestly say that he did a great job with the selections that he made, but I wasn't thrilled about the color so of course I went into my "wife/expert decorator roll". I loved the furniture that Clifton picked, but I insisted that he change the color because what he picked clashed with the colors that were in the living room. So after 20 minutes of me trying to explain why he had to change the color of the furniture he finally gave in, but only after he said "so I guess you'll be paying for all of this?" and I said "no, I got half no worries. He picked the tables and yes they were beautiful, but there was one particular table that I just had to have because it would make my envisioned living room complete.

  I begged and pleaded with Clifton but he constantly told me no! The salesman that was helping us pulled Clifton to the side and asked "is that your wife"? Clifton said "yes". The salesman proceeded to say "Listen you might as well let her go ahead and get the table because telling her no is going to place you in the pits of hell. Trust me I know because I just went through this with my wife about 3 week ago. I'll work out a good price for you; because brother we have to stick together." The salesman walked off and laughed saying that he'll be back with a price. Clifton was looking at the chair that came with the couch;

I actually loved the chair so I had to make him love it to. I politely walked over to him and said "Baby that's your chair sit down so I can see how you look in it". Clifton sat in the chair and I went into my "I'll say whatever it takes to make him get that chair speech". I said "Daddy that's your chair, that chair says king of the castle all day long. Babe that chair says when you sit down I will serve you your dinner and anything else you want, plus it will be right in front of big daddy's T.V. and it will be off limits to everyone, even me. I'll even have a sign made that says RESERVED FOR BIG DADDY ONLY" Clifton looked at me and said "Girl please, gone somewhere with that" then he said "but I really do like this chair" and I said yes you do and so do I. Plus babe it goes with the couch we can't leave it. That was really a long but successful shopping event for my honey and I. What made it even better for me is that with a little persuasion I was able to get a free lamp, the other table that I wanted and big daddy got the chair.

The time came for Clifton's pride and joy to be delivered. No I am not talking about a child; I am talking about our home entertainment system. The day that best buy came to the house was the day I thought Clifton turned 10 again. He was so excited; he sat on the couch looking out the window the majority of the day. He put the dogs in the backyard and walked through the house singing, which was terrible because Cliff did not have a singing voice but he sure thought he did. I was so glad when I saw that van that said "Geek Squad" on it I didn't know what to do! I told Clifton that I was going to get out of the way because I had the worst sinus headache, he said oh ok cool and as I went into the bedroom to lay down I had to laugh because he quickly shut the bedroom door. I opened it back up and said "dang you really wanted me out of the way" He laughed and said "aw naw sweetheart it isn't like that" and then shut the bedroom door back. I re-opened it and said to him "remember you don't want holes in the walls". He told me "Trice this is different they can put holes in the walls you can't" I said whatever and shut the bedroom door again.

Once they were done Clifton had this glow about him. He sat in the living room and played with all the gadgets that geek squad just hooked up. I was trying to rest but that came to a complete holt because all I heard was the darn surround sound. Clifton had the volume up as loud as it could go. I got up and asked him was he crazy? He said "NO! But I am feeling my surround sound and I can't wait until the game comes on tonight". This man and is "toys" I was just no match for them. When any game came on, Clifton and or Keyonta controlled the house or should I say the living room. Thank GOD for the other rooms in the house with doors that could be shut.

Being home with the two of them was fun and also a challenge. Both men of the house stood 6 feet and over I had to constantly prove that height didn't mean a thing and that I knew how to handle the both of them. All I had to do with Cliff is to threaten to call his mom and as far as Keyonta went I was his mama and he already knew not to push my buttons but the two of them would always try me anyway. That's what made our household so fun. It was even better when Simone would come over because now it became 2 on 2. Majority of the time when Simone did come over she and I would let the boys have the house or should I say let her daddy have the house because we would go out and Keyonta would be with his friends. I think Cliff got a little jealous at times of me and Simone but hey who cared we were doing our "mom and daughter" thing. Just like Cliff and Keyonta did their "father and son thing.

    I think the only time that Cliff became too much to handle is when he didn't have the proper rest, or when someone made him mad. I remember the first time Clifton and I had a huge "falling out" regarding his daughter, I couldn't believe it. Clifton had worked the previous night and that morning we all slept in late. Simone was up before we were, she came into the room and said "good morning" I said good morning back to her and she went into the living room to watch television. She later came back to see if her dad was woke and I asked her was she hungry and she said yes. So I told her that I would be up in a minute so I could fix us something to eat. Before I got up I was playing around with Cliff and told him "You are terrible father it is almost

12:00 in the afternoon and you haven't fed your daughter" I laughed and said, "Its ok you don't have to feed my baby I'll do it myself" Oh My God! Why did I say that? Again I was only teasing him. Clifton sat up in the bed and start yelling "What do you mean I'm a terrible father? She didn't even tell me she was hungry". He threw the covers off of him and sat on the side of the bed. I said to him "Clifton calm down, I was only playing with you". "No you weren't you were serious" he got up and stormed off into the kitchen. "If she had of told me she was hungry I would have gotten up to fix her something to eat". I told him "she didn't tell me she was hungry I asked her". He was so in up roar that it was working my nerve. I was in the kitchen making breakfast and he came in screaming at Simone. "Simone if you were hungry why didn't you tell me?" Simone said to her dad, "I didn't tell Trice I was hungry she asked me if I was hungry and I said yes" I looked at Clifton and said "stop raising your voice at her. I told you I asked her, what is your problem? Clifton wasn't trying to hear nothing I was saying or what his daughter had just told him. She was looking at him like she wanted to cry and he was still going at it. "If you were hungry you should have told me, you come and ask or tell me anything else you want". Simone said again "But daddy I didn't tell Trice I was hungry" but he still didn't believe her. I don't know what was wrong with him that morning but he was totally out of line and out of control.

When Simone was done eating she went back into the living room to watch television. I asked Clifton if I could speak to him downstairs, and he agreed. Once downstairs I asked him what was his problem? Why was it such an issue that I asked Simone if she was hungry? Clifton looked at me and said; "yeah that's what you say, but I know that you're taking up for her". I looked at him and said "taking up for her why would we both lie? I did ask her if she was hungry because it was close to noon and I don't know how long she had been up but I kind of figured that she was hungry because hell I was. What was the big deal if she told me she was hungry or if I asked her?

Clifton said "It's not the fact that you asked her, but she could have come and told me". Baby you were still sleeping I said to him. You had just got home at 2:00 this morning. Yeah but still he said. Yeah but still what was my reply. Clifton said because she my daughter. When he said that it felt like he physically slapped me in the face. I sat on the couch and just held my head because I couldn't believe that he said that. I got up because my feelings were torn. I went back up stairs and started throwing some stuff in a bag I had no clue as to where I was going but I knew that I had to get out of the house. As I was getting my bag together Clifton came up stairs into the bedroom where I was, he asked what was I doing and where did I think I was going. In order for me not to go completely off on him I ignored him and continued to pack my bag. I still had the keys to my apartment but there was literally nothing in it but I could still go there.

    I had to think about what I was doing because soon I wouldn't have keys to an apartment, and walking away from the problem that we had wouldn't work either. We were both adults soon to be husband and wife. We were going to have problems big and small and somehow, some way we were going to work them out even if they did piss me off to the point of me wanting to throw something at him. Of course there were going to be times when he felt the same about me.

So instead of me leaving I went out on the back porch and just prayed. I asked GOD to grant me the strength and the right words to speak to Clifton. I was on that back porch talking to myself for a while. "Girl look get it together, Clifton will have these mood swings until he retires hell even after he retires he's a damn policeman". I still couldn't believe that he said "she's my daughter" we never put titles on the kids it was just our kids. Cliff came out onto the porch where I was. He tapped my shoulder and asked was I ok. I turned to him and said "Mr. Lewis you really hurt my feelings. I can't believe that you threw the fact that Simone is your daughter in my face then you acted like she did something wrong if she did tell me she was hungry; Cliff I thought we were supposed to be in this together". I paused for a minute then said to him can I ask to you a question hypothetical of course? He looked at me for a second then said "what is it sweetheart". My question to him was this: What is a woman supposed to do when she has a good man and knows deep down in her heart that he's a good man, who she will climb hills and mountains for, will do any and everything for him with no questions asked. But every time she does anything for him or wants to do anything for him to keep him happy and uplifted he pushes her away. What is she supposed to do? He walked up behind me and pulled me into his arms and said "Keep Pushing eventually he'll get it and he does appreciate it. He also apologized and said that he was frustrated and tired and admitted that he did get out of hand.

The answer that he gave was exactly what I was hoping to hear. With a small sigh I said to him "Thank you, but Cliff you can't always use the fact that you are tried or exhausted as your excuse. If that's the case then every time you're tired or frustrated will you take it out on me or whoever else is in the house at the time"? Still in his arms he looked down at me and said "No I'm not, so don't think like that. Trice thank you for being you. I know you love my daughter I mean "our" daughter and I promise I'll do better".

One thing that I can say about Clifton is that he was very affectionate when we had a disagreement and he knew he was wrong. That was the part of the disputes that I loved, the makeup part. He pulled me even tighter and said "If I see you packing a bag again it better be because we are going on vacation or something" I look up at him and said "Is that a threat"? He looked down at me and said "No I would never do that but pack another bag and see what's going to happen". I laughed and kissed him and told him that I loved him. What he said next sent chills all through me I couldn't believe it. He said "**I Love you too Ms. Tucker.** I was in a state of shock because I could never get him to say that. He would always say yeah yeah when I told him I loved him. God truly answered my prayers that day so I will never ever say that prayer doesn't work!

PROUD MOMENTS!

"That's my boy" is what Cliff would always tell people about Keyonta. It really is indescribable the relationship that Clifton and Keyonta had. They had this bond that shocked me, but one that I was so proud of. There would be times that they would be talking and I would walk into the room and the conversation would just stop; so I being the "nosy one" would always ask "so what are you two talking about? Their response would be "Father and son stuff why"? I guess that was their way of saying to me politely "stay out of our business". Seeing them together made my dreams of family complete.

As I stated before Clifton made sure to be at some if not all of Keyonta basketball games and any other event that he was involved in. Keyonta's senior year in high school we found out that he had been nominated for a full 4 year academic scholarship through the Posse Foundation. Clifton was one of the first people that Keyonta told and Clifton's response was "Son I am so proud of you, that's what's up" Clifton talked about that often he even teased me at times saying "you know he gets his smarts from me, no disrespect to his father but he gets it from me". I would just shake my head and let him have his moment because everyone knows that Keyonta gets everything from his mama.

    The night of the scholarship award ceremony Clifton was more excited than I was. He told Keyonta that he had the scholarship in the bag and not to worry. When we got to the ceremony Keyonta had to go with the other nominees while Clifton, my mother and I found out seats. Upon finding our seats the funniest thing happened. I sat down, my mother sat down but when Clifton tried to sit in the auditorium style seats he couldn't. I tried really hard not to laugh but I couldn't help it. Clifton had to have the end seat and his legs literally had to hang over the two seats that were in front of us because there was not enough space for his legs to fit. Thank God no one was sitting there. Although he was so uncomfortable, the smile that came upon his face when they called Keyonta's name for **Denison University in Granville Ohio** was one that I'll never forget. You would have thought the boy just got drafted to the Chicago Bulls or something but anything that could put a smile upon Cliff face brought a smile to mine as well.

After the ceremony a luncheon was held so parents could meet faculty and staff of the University and other parents of some of the other students who would be attending Denison as well. Each person that Keyonta introduced us to got the following intro: This is my mom Latrice and my Dad Cliff. Without skipping a beat everyone looked at Clifton and then back at Keyonta and said "Wow Keyonta you and your dad tower's over your mom. I just laughed and said "yeah, they do. So that's why I always stand right where I am, in the middle". Everyone told Clifton how they liked Keyonta and how he has raised a good kid. We never said that Clifton was his step-dad, and again no disrespect to Keyonta's father but no one had to know anything more than what they did. Keyonta said on a number of occasions to me that he didn't look at Cliff as a step-dad he thought of him as his "dad" which was fine by the both of us.

I never thought that I would see the day when my son would adapt to another man other than his father and his uncles the way he did with Clifton. Maybe it was because they were the same sign (Taurus) their birthdays were 2 days apart May 5th Cliff and May 7th Keyonta. Maybe it was because Keyonta saw the same thing that I saw in Clifton his beautiful sprit and his kind heart and a great person in general and most importantly Keyonta knew that Cliff made his mom happy.

Keyonta would sometimes go to Cliff before he would come to me if he had problems. I would ask him why didn't he come to me? He would just say "because mom, pops knows better than you do" which translated to me as "girl problems". I remember Clifton telling me one day that Keyonta was going to make the both of us so proud. We will be sitting in the stands at all of his college games, and maybe one day in the stands of an NBA game when he makes it to the pros. I thought that would be great and the plus side to all of that would be that we wouldn't have to hire security because his "pops" would be already standing guard.

Clifton always spoke so highly of Keyonta and Simone; you couldn't tell him anything about his kids. I would laugh though when it came to Simone because these were always his words "Why does she act like that?" I would have to tell him "Baby she's a girl, a pre-teen girl at that and sometimes girls can be a little bit challenging especially to a dad that's a police officer and who has little to no patients what so ever! Simone knew how to push her dad's buttons but she also knew that she had him wrapped around her finger.

Clifton placed his kids on a pedal stool which was great but he worked my nerve when he would tell me "Sweetheart he's a young man let him be". But when I said that same thing about Simone he would blow up. I thought to myself "What the hell is he going to do when she's starts dating"? Yes that conversation came up many times only because Keyonta was at what I called the "dating age". I did get a little jealous when he would talk to Cliff about certain things and not me but I am so glad that he had such a positive influence and someone that he felt comfortable enough to talk to.

Graduation was approaching for Keyonta, June 2011 to be exact. We had so much to do prom, his trunk party, visiting Denison, taking him to Denison and Clifton was ready. I think that he was more excited than I was. Of course Keyonta brought his potential prom dates home so we could meet them and "pops" gave him thumbs up or the real quick shake of the head which meant NO! Typical let mom do all of the running while pops gives all the advice.

Two weeks before Keyonta's Prom I will admit that Cliff did do a little running around with me and I was so glad because I was becoming so frustrated. I kept saying to him "Cliff this is not right, I am running around like a chicken with my neck cut off for our son not our daughter, so if it's like this for him we are in trouble when Simone goes on prom because the work is going to triple" and his answer to that was simply "No it's not because she's not going to prom" Oh My GOD! Was all I could say. Clifton told me that I made everything harder than it actually was. Again I hated when he was right but I wanted everything to be perfect for my baby but yet again Cliff in dad mode said calm down we got this. He arranged for Keyonta's limousine, he gave half for his pre-prom party and he picked up his shoes because we had them custom made to complete his prom attire.

Prom day came and boy was I glad when it was over but mister cool took everything in stride and made sure that his son was taken care of. He gave Keyonta the "Father/son lecture slid a couple dollars in his pockets and pulled me away from the car. Clifton made that day and the days to come so special for Keyonta and I.

The day of Keyonta's graduation, although exhausted because he worked the night before Clifton was dressed and rushing me. He had the camera ready and his pride and chest all front and center.

Keyonta was a national honor society student and ranked number 10 out 121 students. Because he was a part of the national honor society they went up first to receive their diplomas. When they called his name I think Clifton, my mom, and the rest of the family were the loudest people in the auditorium. All Clifton kept saying was yeah that's my boy, that's my boy. I tapped him on the shoulder and said "baby I think everyone in here knows that by now" but that was only after I made that announcement myself several times.

Later on that evening after everything was over Clifton and I were at home he said to me "Trice today was one of the best days of my life, I saw my son walk across the stage." Ok there went my emotions again trying not to cry I simply said "Mr. Lewis yes you did and you know what, I got a feeling that you will see your son walk across several more stages. Just wait until he walks across the stage receiving his Bachelors and Masters and maybe even his PHD". Clifton said "yeah Sweetheart I can't wait".

August 15th 2011 we packed Keyonta up and headed towards Granville Ohio to Denison University. Not only was that the proudest moment of my life but the most memorable one ever. It was a 5 to 6 hour drive and trust me Clifton wasn't a high way driver but that day he drove the entire trip. He said "Sweetheart I remember when my mom and her friend were doing this for me". About 3 hours into our trip Clifton called his mother and said to her "Hey Ma guess what I am doing? I am on the road taking my son to school. It's a good feeling now I see how you felt when you were driving me down to JSU" (Jackson State

University). Only GOD and I knew how my heart felt that day and as long as I live I will never forget those words. All I could do was thank God for placing such a wonderful man not only in my life but also in the life of my son. After he got off the phone with his mother I leaned over and kissed him on the cheek and said softly to him I LOVE YOU! And thank you so much! He just looked over at me with a small smile and said yeah, yeah (I truly wanted to hear I love you too but yeah yeah was close enough).

Finally we arrived. Clifton and I both were like Wow! Although I had already seen the campus Cliff hadn't so his comment was "man this is a nice campus but I didn't know that it sat on top of a hill". As we were driving up to admissions, room and board I said "Keyonta all I can say is you are going to have some strong legs and calves". Before we started unloading Keyonta's things we stopped one of the students to ask for assistance. She approached us and said to me "Hi, Welcome to Denison do you need help finding something?" I was so flattered because she thought that I was the college student so I played right along with it. She asked me was this my first year and told me that I was going to love it there. Keyonta and Cliff looked at me like really! Clifton said to me "Sweetheart stop it, and he then said to the young lady she's not the student our son is". She looked at me then looked back at Keyonta and said really, he's your son. At that point my fun was over and I had to actually admit that Keyonta was the student. I enjoyed every moment, because that only proved that I still look as young as I feel. Of course Keyonta cleared things up when he also said "She my mother and this is my dad" and the young lady said to the both of us "Wow you two don't look like you have a college age son" Clifton smiled and said thanks, then turned to me and said "Guess I still got it too now deal with that". I laughed and said to him "She was only referring to me; she just didn't want to hurt your feelings that's why she said you two". The look on Clifton's face was indescribable; but yes you could see that he was a proud papa. After Keyonta was all settled in he kicked me and Cliff off campus but before we left Clifton pulled him to the side and told him to call him and let him know if he needed anything else and we would get it before we leave. When we got back to the hotel we were both exhausted from climbing 4 flights of stairs and of course driving for 6 ½ hours. Tired as I was I could do nothing but hug and hold him because Clifton had no idea how grateful, thankful, just how humble I was to have him in our lives. I told him that I was so lucky; God blessed me with some one that I had been waiting on for so long. I told him that I didn't know how I could ever repay him for all the things that he has done. Clifton at first looked at me like I was losing my mind, but then he hug me so tight and told me that everything was going to be alright and that he was the lucky one.

Later on that night Clifton received a phone call. He got up and walked into the bathroom and stayed in there for a minute or two. Yes my mind got to wondering but I don't know why because I have never had any concerns about who he talked to on his phone but this time I wanted to know who is he talking to and why did he have to go into the bathroom to talk to them. So I got up and went to the bathroom door and sad "Who are you talking to that you had to leave the room"? He looked at me and smiled. I didn't think it was funny so I asked again this time he said to the person on the phone "Look my wife is getting jealous and she wants to know who I am talking too so could you please do me a favor and say hello to her.

At first I thought he was making fun of me which made me even madder, so to get back at him I snatched his phone and said "HELLO!" The person on the phone said "Hey ma why you all worried about who pops is talking to"

I looked at the phone and then looked up a Clifton he was so red from laughing. "That's what you get. Sweetheart I don't know how many times I have to tell you that you are the only fool that wants me" and he laughed some more.

The following morning we got up and head out to Wal-Mart. Keyonta had given Clifton a list of things that he didn't have and to my surprise I knew nothing about this list until we got to the store and he pulled it out. Although I do remember Clifton telling Keyonta to let him know if he needed anything else but I never knew he gave him a list. I looked at it and ask when did he get that? His response was "Tamara Tucker stay in your lane don't worry about when I got this". So as he asked I stayed in my lane and didn't say another word until we got to the checkout. Clifton turned to me and said "Sweetheart I need 10 dollars". I said "really, I could give you this ten dollars but you told me to stay in my lane remember" with laughter I handed him the ten dollars. We went back to campus to drop Keyonta's things off to him. We didn't stay long but while we were there Cliff the "animal lover" came across a family of deer he literally stop the truck and got out with his cell phone in hand taking pictures and talking to the deer. I politely stayed inside the truck rolled my window down and said the first one that charges I am pulling off.

On the trip back home I know Clifton got tired of me thanking him but I couldn't help it. He helped make my (our) son's transition from high school to college a smooth and enjoyable one. Although one baby was away at school I still had two more at home with me. Clifton was one and Simone being the other. My family, the family that I always knew I would have was now complete. Clifton and I were mapping everything out, one child off to college and one more to go. We started writing down all of the vacation spots we were going to hit once both kids were gone and out of our pockets of course it was unlikely that the both of them (Keyonta and Simone) being out of our pockets would ever happen but hey we both were dreamers.

Clifton started working on his man cave and his garage. I had limits to what I could and could not do in his "spaces". He explained to me that he knew that I would take over the entire house but the basement (man cave) and his garage was off limits. The only people that were aloud in those two places were him, his guys, his son, his dogs and that darn cat FIONA! No women were aloud. That was fine by me. I informed him that since the washer and dryer was in the basement which was now his man cave and I am a woman who wasn't allowed the laundry would now become his job on the regular. He laughed and said "Sweetheart there's an exception to every rule". I hoped that this exception to every rule thing worked in my favor as well especially for the holiday.

The holidays were the best for us, well for me anyway. I always wanted to have family over so I made a big fuss about it. Thanksgiving and Christmas were my favorites. For two years straight I won the battle for Thanksgiving but trust me they were hard fought battles. Clifton asked "Why do you always want people over?" I know that I have stated several times that Mr. Lewis was a very private person and I always respected that, but again being from a large family I was just use to having lots of family around especially for the holidays. So like I said I won the Thanksgiving holiday but Christmas was a different story.

Clifton told me period point blank "We are not having company over for Christmas; as a matter of fact I don't have a problem with you going to your grandma's for Christmas". That was a major blow for me because Cliff knew that I wanted to be around both our families with him. We even had a bigger dispute over the Christmas tree I wanted a tree put up and he didn't. He said over and over again "Sweetheart we are not putting up a tree there is no need for all of that the kids are not babies anymore and a tree would only take up space.

Well I didn't care about space or the fact that the kids were not babies, a tree was going up and all of the other decorations as well. We went on for days before a decision was finally made. After me bickering and pouting Clifton finally said "Listen Tamara I'll let you put that artificial tree up this time but next year and the years on out the only tree that will be in this house will be a live pine tree do you understand me"? I looked at him like he was crazy then I said to him "No! We will not have a live tree because I am not cleaning up all those darn pine needles and plus I don't like the way they smell they stink".

Now mind you I said all of this sitting down. Clifton walked over to the couch stood over me and said "you heard what I said Ms. Tucker". Before I could gave a response back Clifton put his hand up to my mouth and said "Shush don't say another word big daddy has spoken a live tree next year period!" In all honesty that was hilarious but me being the "obedient soon to be wife" I left it alone. But in the back of my mind I was saying "His ass will be the one cleaning up those damn stinky needles since he's the one that wants a live tree".

MY OH MY GOD MOMENTS

Happiness was all over me. I have never felt the way I was feeling. We were getting our home together, our kids were good, and the best thing ever (I hoped) was soon to happen. As I stated a few chapters back I had to threaten Clifton about marriage; well not really threaten but I did stress the issue of marriage a whole lot.

He knew for a fact that I wasn't budging, he was stuck with me for the rest of his life. I told him that I was going to be the one smashing his peas at dinner time or always making mashed potatoes when it was time for him to wear dentures. He would always laugh and say to me "yeah ok I think you got it twisted I will be the one smashing your peas. I didn't pay for these braces for me to have bad teeth when they come off". I have no clue as to what braces had to do with anything but hey I always rolled with the punches because Mr. Lewis was always right (at least he thought he was).

Clifton and I spoke more openly about marriage which I was very pleased about. He was very low key with everything. Unlike me who wanted to tell the world that in less than a year I would be marrying the love of my life. **I most definitely have to thank my mother-in-law Maxine** because if it wasn't for her constantly telling Clifton "son don't let what happen in your past stop you from letting someone else love you" I think I would have gone crazy.

For a long time Clifton said that he wasn't getting married, he wasn't the marrying type, marriage wasn't for him, and anything thing else that had the word marriage in it did not applied to him. After a long fought battle of the mind Clifton said that if he "were to get married" he would do a destination wedding which would have been fine for me (because now he was even thinking marriage) but everyone couldn't afford to travel and to be truthful about it we couldn't either but I think we would have found a way.

After I talked him out of that I put plan B in to place. I have always said that if I got married it would be one time and one time only. I wanted a nice wedding and reception, something that both of our families could enjoy and be involved in. Clifton was totally against that why I didn't know but that wasn't going to stop me for having the dream wedding that I wanted with the man of my dreams.

For a while we really didn't talk too much more about getting married. We focused more on maintaining the house, making sure the kids were ok and me completing school. Clifton even mentioned a couple of times that he wanted to go back to school himself to get his Master's Degree in Business.

I supported that idea because it would have actually cut back on all that darn working Clifton did. I asked him several times "are you Jamaican" because he held so many jobs. He would laugh and say "no but if there is money out there to be made why shouldn't I make it". He supported the fact that I was continuing my education. He sometimes would stay up at night with me and help me go over some assignments. He would also be the one who would "pull the plug" when he saw me trying to study and my head going back and forward from exhaustion. He would say "Sweetheart you worked all day and you have to be back up in a couple of hours to be back at work that's enough".

I have always been a determined person but I think Clifton made me even more determined and focused because he gave me 100% of his support and was there to cheer me on. He would always tease me saying "You talk about me do you ever stop school, work, taking care of us and everybody else. "Sweetheart when are you going to realize that you can't do it all".

So many times I had to tell him to take his own advice. "You need to learn how to say no when someone asks you if you want to do a side gig" but it never worked. Simply put Clifton was a workaholic it was just in his nature and I can honestly say and I quote "he got from his mama". He was so glad when she retired. He always gave her such a hard time when she would go in on her off days. He would say "mama that's enough you've served your time in the work force now it's time for you to sit down". Again, how I wished he took his own advice.

July 2011 we all went out to my aunt Pier's house for her annual 4th of July celebration. As we were enjoying the fireworks my aunt Pier walked over to Clifton and said "So when are you guys going to city hall I am so ready for a reception or something". Clifton said to her "I'll go tomorrow but your niece is insisting on having an overpriced wedding". I heard everything and replied "No I do not want to go to city hall and no I don't want an overpriced wedding. But I do want him to see me walk down the aisle, I do want my father to give me away, and I don't think anything is wrong with that". Pier said "Cliff she is not the boss of you, you should put your foot down and make her butt go to city hall".

Cliff looked at me and I looked back at him and said "Babe don't listen to her, listen to the person that you have to go home with". Clifton just held his head down and said I have nothing to say and continued to eat his ribs.

It's funny because on the way home we did sort of touch on the subject. Clifton did ask again why was it so important to me to have a wedding instead of just going to city hall. Cliff knew why I didn't want to go to city hall but I explained it to him again. "Cliff going to city hall meant to me that we were going to get married just to say we are married to make that little piece of paper that says marriage licenses valid. I want to have a nice ceremony that would let people know that the vows that we will be reciting will be forever and that they were being said before the eyes and ears of God and those whom we love and those who love us. Plus its every girls dream to one day wear a beautiful wedding dress and let her new hubby lift her veil after the pastor pronounce them man and wife, at least it's my dream". I got quite for a moment and looked at Clifton again and said "Do you really want to go to city hall? If that's what you really want then fine we can" then I looked back out the window.

I guess by the tone in my voice he knew that wasn't what I wanted to do so he said "No we are going to have this wedding that you want" as he kind of nudged me. I look at him again and asked "why did you say it like that, this wedding? It's not right if it's not a mutual thing between the two of us, as a matter of fact why we don't just forget about it. I told you that I didn't want to feel like I was pressuring you to get married and the way you just said that makes me feel like I am pressuring you.

I know that he heard the aggravation in my voice and the look on my face didn't make it any better. Clifton said to me "Trice you're not pressuring me". I think at that point he was becoming aggravated as well so I said to him again, "let's not talk about it right now let's change the subject". He insisted and said "No we are going to talk about it. Because if we don't you will have an attitude and right now I really don't feel like dealing with you and a attitude". I knew he was right but I responded "No I won't have an attitude so just drop it".

Then out the blue he said set a date! Was I hearing him correctly? Did he just say set a date? He turned the radio down and said "You heard me yes I said set a date". Before I knew it, I said "October 14, 2012". Cliff looked at me like I was crazy and said "October why October, is it because that's your birthday month"? Ok it was a little truth to that, but that wasn't the reason. "No mister knows it all! It's because it's cheaper and I love the fall colors".

The ride home that night seemed like it took forever. We went back and forth about that date but in the end I won that. Over excited when we got home I wanted some "very affectionate" time with Clifton but he said "Get away from me what happen to the attitude you just had"? "I never had an attitude you just thought I did". He said to me "you did have an attitude and if you touch me again I am going to scream rape then tell everyone that you put my gun to my head and told me that if I didn't marry you, you were going to kill me." My response to that was "Rape? Big as you are I raped you". Who's gonna believe you? Plus everyone that knows me, know that I HATE guns so that gun lie won't fly and size does matter so rape won't either. He laughed and said to me "Trust me I have ways to making people believe me."

As the months went by I started doing a little planning behind the scenes which Clifton knew nothing about. I did show him a few things every now and then but the majority of the small stuff I did on my own. We argued about the colors, I wanted yellow summer set mixed with a touch of orange, and cream (yellow or cream was to be the colors of my bridesmaids dresses and the orange was to be the color of their flowers) Clifton said no to the orange and yellow. He said "my wedding colors are going to be cranberry and cream" and I said "NO! I am not having dark colors in my wedding". He literally threw it in my face when he said "Oh remember what you said it's not your wedding it's our wedding so with that being said cranberry and cream it is". Of course I wasn't going for that, so in order to put things in prospective for the both of us I ordered a lot of color swatches from bubble gum pink to eggplant purple. I was praying that he would see it may way and go with the lighter colors. (Remember he said I was spoiled, well he wasn't lying about that but he made me this way).

One evening he came in from work to find color swatches all over the bed. "Trice what is all of this"? He asked. I said to him "Colors that we can choose from for OUR wedding because I am not doing cranberry". Now I am all for the cream but that damn cranberry has got to go. He moved the swatches to the other side of the bed and said "I am tired and I am going to bed". For about 2 weeks he paid no attention to those swatches. I didn't make a big fuss about it because in the back of my mind I knew how all of this was going to turn out. He was going to let me have my way and he would complain about it later.

<u>God Answered My Prayers</u>

A month went past and we finally started discussing rings. Clifton told me that he was not breaking the bank for my ring which was fine by me, but I explained to him that the ring that he did get better had looked like he spent a year's salary on it. I wasn't a hard person to please and he knew it but my finger had to represent my hard fought battle. We didn't have a budget for the rings but we did agree that we wouldn't go overboard. Although if I had to for him I was willing to go above and beyond but I wouldn't tell him that because he wouldn't allow it period!!

We looked at several different rings all of them were very beautiful pieces but none of them jumped out at me. None of them said "Mrs. Clifton P. Lewis forever" so the search continued. I thought that I would find my ring by my birthday but that didn't happen instead I got dinner, a movie, and a beautiful bath filled with rose petals.

I was shocked! Never in a million years would I have guessed that Mr. Lewis had this type of romantic bone in his body. Yes intimacy was out of this world ALL OF THE TIME! But Clifton rarely did "romantic, spontaneous stuff" like the rose petals he was too darn reserved and laid back. I will say that Clifton showed me something different on several occasions and you better believe that there were never any complaints from me but the rose petals were still a shocker.

Clifton and I were in a good place and happy with our new lives. I say new because that's just what it was. New home, getting use to new things (i.e.: living together), and him saying this is my wife instead of my girl and me saying this is my husband instead of my guy. I sometimes even got Cliff to go to church with me but if it was football season and he was off that Sunday he would simply say to me "Sweetheart God knows my heart and he also knows that I want to chill and watch the game" I would move to the side and look up and say "Lord please let me be out of the way when you throw that lightning bolt". Clifton didn't have to go to church for me to know that he was a God fearing man. That's why I never really made a big deal out of it. As a matter of fact the second date that Clifton and I went on was to United Baptist Church under the leadership of Dr. Rev. Wilson Daniels.

His biggest frustration and the one that weighted heavy on the both of us was him not being able to spend a lot of time with his daughter. Two things played major parts for him not being able to see her like he wanted to. One was his work schedule and the second was the unease conflicts he would have with his daughter's mother. Clifton's work schedule was terrible but that's what it was being that he was a Chicago police officer. Sometimes he would work 7am to 3pm, 6pm to 2am, 8am to 5pm and sometimes it was even worse than that if there was something going on. Did I like his schedule no, but I did tease him all the time telling him that his work schedule was the reason I was marrying him. The way our work schedules ran was like this, if he was going I was coming and vice versa so when we were at home together sometimes it would be like our first date again but with a lot of perks, **censored** perks!   Cliff would always say "I got 8 more years and then I am calling it quits". I knew for a fact that he was lying. It was in Clifton's blood to work and be a strong provider so sitting him down wasn't going to be an easy task.

In regards to the conflicts that Cliff had with his daughters mother I can, but I won't go into those issues because that's not for me to do, but I will say that I was frustrate with a lot of it. I was at the point where I just got tired of trying to figure her out. I can only go off of the things that Clifton told me, and some of those things were not nice. The only thing I knew about Simone's mother personally was her name and that she had two other daughters but the more he told me the less I wanted to know. I even started having doubts about meeting her but with all due respects in a matter of months I was going to be her daughters step-mother so that was the only and main reason I had for wanting to meet her. Clifton was a great father who did everything he could for his daughter but I guess it wasn't good enough for his daughter's mother because he always received so much negativity from her.

Each time an altercation took place and Clifton told me about it I'd be ready to contact Simone's mother myself but Clifton would always tell me to just let it be. He just didn't know how hard that was for me to do knowing that she would upset him to the point where he wanted to knock a hole in the wall. I never felt as helpless as I did when he would tell me "just let it be". I really wanted to meet his daughter mother because I needed to see the person that brought a beautiful child into the world but caused so much grief to the person that helped to make that possible. When I would ask Clifton what was his reason for me not meeting her he just said "Trice there's no need for you to meet her, as long as **I KNOW** that my daughter is being taken care of when she's with you nothing else matters".

There were countless times when I would be angry and upset with Keyonta's dad but Cliff would always tell me that everything was going to be ok, don't let that upset you. So many times I wondered why he never took his own advice.

I found that to be so unfair because as a parent myself I needed or should I say I wanted to know the people or persons that my son's father had in his life and they needed to know who Keyonta's mother was. I didn't have a problem with anyone being in my son's life as long as they never disrespected him and most importantly never mistreated him. I wanted Cliff to meet Keyonta's father out of respect for the both of them. It was important for Keyonta's father to know the man that would forever play a major role in his son's life and that's why I made it an issue to meet Simone's mother. I wanted to let her know that before I am anything I am a **PARENT** and from the moment I started dating Clifton Simone became my daughter. Clifton never raised his voice, cursed or said anything harsh until the last time I asked to meet Simone's mother. "Why in the hell do you keep asking to meet her? I told you there is no damn need for you to meet her so stop asking". After that I guess you can say that he got his point across and I stop asking. I just humbly submitted myself to Clifton's wishes. I left it alone and stopped questioning his reasons.

Everything was going in the right direction for our family. Keyonta was loving and doing great in his first year of college, Clifton was working on ways to spend more time with Simone and I was still working on making our wedding plans official. Clifton and I got invited to one of his fellow officer's wedding; I do believe that this was the wedding that made his decision about us getting married final. On our way home that evening Clifton said to me "Ms Tucker I think that I am ready to make you Mrs. Lewis you said October 2012 right"? I was speechless for about 5 minutes I had to make sure that I heard him correctly. Again he triggered my emotions because my eyes were blurred from tearing, yes he made me cry a lot but it was always for wonderful reasons. I couldn't believe it; I was trying to figure out what brought this about? He replied "You've twisted my arm enough I'm ready"

There was a huge sigh from me and I responded "Mr. Lewis I am ready to become Mrs. Lewis, I was ready to be Mrs. Lewis the moment I met you". Of course Clifton had a smart remark to say and he always knew how to mess up the moment. "Really, you wanted to be Mrs. Lewis from the time you met me? How is that possible when you didn't even know my name until I told it to you?" So with his smart remark came mine "You didn't have to tell me your name, I read it off your name tag that was on your darn vest that night". Again he had a comeback answer, "yeah my name was on the tag that you saw on my vest that night, but it only said my last name, so I did have to tell you what my name was".

I was so excited and overwhelmed. I couldn't believe that Cliff actually admitted that he was ready to get married. Don't think that I didn't stay on his back after that. There were times where we would be in bed and I would have my laptop and we would look at halls and certain designs, but when he got tired of it he would say to me "Trice why do I need to look at all this stuff? No matter what I say two things always happen you don't like what I pick and eventually you'll try to talk me into to changing my mind so why do we even go through this?"

Sad to say it but he was absolutely correct. I guess he knew that what I wanted I was going to get (at least those were my thoughts anyway). Secretly I think Clifton was excited as well but because he was the "MAN" he couldn't or he wouldn't let that be known. He would just say, "Sweetheart at this point it's all about you and basically all I have to do is be there with the ring and say I do". That wasn't true at all I wanted him to be so involved in every single aspect of our wedding because it was not just about me it was about us, it was about our new beginning as a family as man and wife as God intended for us to be.

He would always joke with me and say his biggest part was his wallet and making sure everything was paid for and I would jokingly say "Mr. Lewis your wallet wouldn't fit my budget". Of course he always had snappy come backs; he said to me "Well you better get a couple more gigs if my wallet can't fit your budget. You know you are not too good to flip a burger or two". At that point I just came to the conclusion that Clifton was crazy and I overlooked all those crazy remarks and crazy comments and told him regardless to what he said our wedding was going to be one to remember.

It was around November 2011 I started getting excited about a few things and Thanksgiving was one of them. I knew that I was going to argue with Cliff about having family over and about the Christmas tree but I didn't care I was ready. It was tradition for me to put my Christmas tree up two days after Thanksgiving or even the day after it didn't matter, but I wasn't too happy about the fact that this year I had to have darn live tree. Why do I have to put up with the stinky smell of pine all through my house? Heck the only pine that I will put up with is pine sol!

For the record yes I did get the lecture about family coming over to the house and because I wanted family over he got his stinking live tree. Comprising was the pits sometimes.

November was also the time that Clifton took vacation but for some strange reason he never really told me he was on vacation. I would get up for work and he wouldn't, and I would come home from work and he'd still be home. This would go on for about two days until I would ask "are you on vacation?" He would just smile or smirk and say "what gave it away". I wondered why it was such a big secret about him being on vacation until I finally figured it out; he didn't tell me when he was going on vacation because he knew that I would be quick to book a trip or have something planned for us to do. Having him home was great, but it really was never a "vacation" for him because he would still work his part-time jobs.

Thanksgiving Day was busy but enjoyable for us. Both of our families were here at the house and I can honestly say that when everyone left Clifton and I sat on the couch like we were the oldest people in the world. He turned to me and said "Won't happen next year Ms. Tucker we will be ordering take out". Tired as I was, feet hurting and legs cramping from standing for so long I told Clifton "baby I totally agree. Eventually my mind would change, only after my feet and the rest of my body stop throbbing.

Now that Thanksgiving was over I immediately became filled with the excitement and anticipation of Christmas. I could shop and plus I would have the chance to see if my totes put any fear in Cliff. Okay they didn't but they were surely worth the try. Hell he used one of them for the dog's food. As usual we discussed what we were going to get for the kids and other family members. I didn't have to tell Cliff what I wanted for Christmas, but I did tell him that if my finger wasn't holding a piece that was about a carat in a half I was packing my stuff and leaving. He just laughed and said to me "girl please your spoiled butt ain't going nowhere". **(Damn it! I HATED WHEN HE WAS RIGHT!)**. As I said I knew wanted I for Christmas, but Clifton was the hardest person to shop for because he was a man that had everything and who was really particular about the stuff that was bought for him. I knew for a fact that I was not buying another piece of exercise equipment so his gift was going to be a challenge.

I literally had to ask him time and time again "Baby what would you like for Christmas?" He wouldn't give me a solid answer he would just hunch his shoulders and say I don't know, and yes I went through this every year. I told him I wanted to get him a pool table but he said I couldn't because it was too expensive. I told him cost didn't matter and if I can afford it why couldn't I get it for him? Let me just say that when Clifton said no he meant no. There was no way around it, he meant no.

I had to watch Clifton do certain things to find out or get an idea about what I could get him for Christmas since he always told me no about everything. About three days before Thanksgiving I saw him looking at catalog and he kept saying "I want these boots, I really want these boots".

I asked him why he hadn't got them or why doesn't he get them? He said to me "because no one seems to have my size" and he left it at that. The good part about me being very observant with him was the fact that I saw the boots and thought wow I would knock him off his feet if I get those boots.

A couple of days went past and for some strange reason Clifton became all bubbly and happy. He would come home smiling or always joking about something. I wanted to ask what was wrong but I couldn't bring myself to ask because I was enjoying the care free Clifton, but the happy go lucky Cliff left and the sad and sometimes angry Cliff came back after I got this news.

Clifton always talked about getting rid of the dogs but I would never take him serious because he loved his dogs so much and every time he mentioned he was giving them away I'd just say "Yeah baby whatever you have said that a dozen times and they are still in the same place they were the first thousand times you said it".

Shockingly one day while I was out Keyonta called me and said "Mom don't tell Cliff I called you but when you get home just act like you usually do". The first thing that came to my mind was Clifton bought my ring and he showed it to Keyonta. Oh My God was I excited until he said "Ma, Cliff got rid of the dogs they are gone" of course all of my excitement left. "What do you mean he got rid of the dogs, both of them"? Keyonta said he couldn't believe it either but yes he did, he took them both to a no kill pit bull animal rescue shelter.

Still in disbelief when I got home that evening I noticed Clifton sitting at the foot of the bed bouncing a ball that the dogs once played with. So I politely asked "baby what's up? Why are you playing with the dogs ball, that thing is filthy". When Clifton looked up at me he was all teary eyed and said "They're gone, my boys are gone". I stood in front of him and asked what was he talking about? He just looked and said "I gave them away, fat boy and Spartacus I took them to the shelter.

If you could have seen the hurt in his face it would have torn you apart. I sat next to him rubbed his back and told him that they were going to be okay and then I asked what made him do it? Why did he take them to the shelter? He said that they were beginning to be too much. Clifton knew that I was scared of Spartacus for one and because of his work schedule he felt that they were not being taken care of like they were supposed to be.

I hugged him and told him eventually we can get another dog. What did I say that for? Clifton literally threw me a piece paper with a lot of dogs on it and said "pick one". With the craziest look on my face I said "What, are you serious"? Of course he was serious. He said we can get a puppy and make sure that he is house broken and one that I wouldn't be afraid off and one that would scare off unwanted company. He just didn't know what was going through my head at that moment. I looked at him and said "Mr. Lewis are you for real? We just got rid of two and you are already ready to get another one"? He smiled and said you asked me what I wanted for Christmas.

That wasn't the gift that I had planned on buying and I wasn't too thrilled about getting another dog but to keep down confusion I just said "yeah babe I am not buying a dog, I'll get you anything else but I am not buying a dog". The dog debate went on for about 4 days until Clifton said "Trice you don't have to get me a dog, I'll get one myself". When it came to Clifton and his animals I never tried to argue or make a fuss about it because that was a battle that I would never win, especially after he said "After Christmas we will be getting another dog maybe even two" he was serious so I just threw my hands up and walked off.

At this point it really didn't matter to me because Clifton was well informed that I was not going to be responsible for the dogs so I didn't care. What I did care about was my Christmas gift. Was I going to pout for the next year? Or was I going to glow every day? God the waiting was killing me. Christmas Eve morning I got up and fixed breakfast for the two leading men in my life. After breakfast Cliff told me that we were going to pick up Simone and afterwards we could finish up our last minute shopping, well at least I could because he wasn't one for buying people stuff he would just give money to his nieces and nephews and the same was for his mom and his sister's (I'm hoping they got a little more than the kids).

As we were heading out Clifton gave me the going to the mall rules. He did this every time we went to any store.

He turned to me and said "sweetheart we are not going to every store, it's ok to go to a couple but remember I don't have a problem with taking your checkbook, debit and credit cards so with that being said we're going to keep it moving." Now y'all know I have never paid any attention to him when it came to me shopping but I was mindful on occasion.

Clifton decided that I was driving he said he just wanted to sit back and relax. I didn't have a problem with driving I just always felt that it was proper for him to drive and I look cute on the passenger side but that's another story.

Our morning went from laughing and joking to total insanity and angry words. As we were on our way to pick Simone up; Clifton called her mom to inform her that we were on our way. I don't think it was his intention for me to hear the things that Simone's mother was saying, but I did. As Clifton began his conversation it started out with a simple hi, we are on our way to pick Simme up (Simone's nickname). Let me state again that it wasn't intentional that I heard what was said on the other end of the phone but I did and it took the entire woman of God that I am for me not to comment.

Conversation: We are on our way to pick Simme up.

Who is we?

What do you mean who is we? Me and Trice who else did you think I was talking about?

Oh so now you are father of the year? (Laugh)

Look I didn't call you to argue with you, I just called to let you know that I am on my way.

Anyway, she has to be back in the morning.

What do you mean in the morning? How come she can't stay with me?

Because she can't I want her back home in the morning.

Pausing this ridiculously screwed up conversation. At this point I was over on the driver side boiling and thinking this is some straight bullshit. After hearing what was said, I looked at Cliff and sort of whispered "Baby in the morning? Why do we have to take her back in the morning"? Clifton looked at me and said "Sweetheart let me handle this." Don't get me wrong I wanted to let him handle it but the more they talk the more he started to turn red and the higher my pressure went.

Conversation continued: Again why can't she stay with me? You wouldn't let her come over for Thanksgiving and now you are telling me that she can only stay with me until the morning?

Her: I want her home because we always have breakfast together on Christmas morning at my aunt's house.

Cliff: I understand that but it won't hurt if she's not there, I, I mean we want her with us for Christmas.

Her: Well I said no, you have to bring her home in the morning.

Stopping this childish conversation again. Now we are on the express way and I am driving 75 miles per hour. I wish you could have felt the heat that was coming from my body. As Clifton is going back and forth with his daughter's mother I start talking out loud. "It's might funny how you can be called when she needs money for summer camp, or she needs money for this and that, and you break your damn neck to get it out there to her but when you want to spend time with her it's always a issue. Babe I am tired of this bull shit. It's not fair that you have to go through all this damn drama just to see her". Clifton looked over at me raising his voice "Trice please be quite I said I can handle this" I could not believe that he was raising his voice at me I was so mad that I almost hit the back of the truck that was in front of me.

Conversation cont.

Cliff: Look after these holidays are over we are going to sit down and discuss a schedule especially a holiday schedule of when I can get Simone. I am tired of not being able to get Simme around the holidays, I couldn't get her for the fourth of July because you had something planned, you wouldn't let her come over for Thanksgiving. "Damn will I ever be able to spend one holiday with my daughter".

Her: Cliff I am not trying to hear all of that, just have her back home in the morning.

Before I could say anything else Clifton hung up the phone. She makes me sick; he said as he hit the dash of the car. Although I knew he was mad, I had to say what I felt. "Cliff why do you put up with that? Why is she so unfair? What the hell is her problem? I have never seen anything like her in my life". Cliff sat quietly for a while, tapping his foot, mumbling under his breath then he said, "I am going to file for joint custody, I am sick of this shit".

I couldn't stand when he was mad with his daughter's mother because the back lash of frustration and anger would be directed at me but not intentionally. I could ask a simple question like "Cliff where did you say you put the dryer sheets? He would respond with this aggressive tone of voice.   I would have to remind him that he's directing all that at the wrong person but in the end he would always apologize but who wanted to go through that all the time, I sure as hell didn't.

After picking Simone up we tried to make the atmosphere a little calmer and peaceful. We drove around looking for an IPOD touch for Simone. We went to a few stores and of course every last one that we went to was sold out. Little did I know Cliff had already had the darn thing, but I found that out Christmas morning. Anyway we finally end up at the mall. We went into a few clothing stores, I grabbed a few things and so did Cliff and I couldn't believe that but he did. As we were walking thru the mall Clifton stopped and looked at me and said "I guess that's it we can hit the road" I looked at him and said "uh **NO** Mr. Lewis we're not finished". He looked back at me and said "What, do you need to get something else"? I didn't say a word I just rolled my eyes and started to walk ahead of him. He grabbed my arm and started laughing and said "What's wrong with you?" I didn't respond I just continued to pull away from him. As I was pulling away he said "Girl quit acting like that" and then walked into Kay's Jewelry store, you know the one with the cute little jingle "Every kiss begins with Kay's".

Okay I can't lie, that whole frown/attitude thing that I had going on vanished. The smile that came across my face felt like the sun had just rose and its rays were warming me. I couldn't let him know of my excitement so I calmly walked into the jewelry store and began to browse a bit. Simone and I were looking at rings and Clifton was looking at earrings. Once he was done he came over to where Simone and I were looked at me and said "Sweetheart you are looking in the wrong case I am not paying that much money for a ring. You need to come back over to this case the one that says CLEARENCE!"

Of course I looked at him like he was crazy. I had my heart set on this one ring that just felt like it was calling my name but Clifton pointed again to the clearance case. With a lot of hesitation I finally went over to the case where he was standing. Don't get me wrong there were some nice rings in the clearance case and I did see two that sort of caught my attention. But they must have really caught Clifton's eye when I showed them to him because he never moved from that case. He liked the two I showed him because he asked me which one I liked best, I picked one from the two but again my heart was set on another. Clifton sat on the little stool and said "Sweetheart your pouting is not going to work. You can stop looking in that other case because like I said I am not paying that much money for a ring". Still eyeing the ring that I wanted but could not get, Clifton gave the salesmen the ring that I chose from the clearance case, but oh how I beg to try the ring on that was in the other case.

After about 3 minutes of begging Clifton allowed me to try the ring on. He said that it was a really nice ring with a really nice price on it. I looked at him and said "Babe this is the one, this is the one that says Mrs. Clifton Lewis for eternity. He looked at it and said "Yeah okay, now take it off". I was so mesmerized by this ring that I never wanted it to come off my finger. I mean I didn't have to have it sized or anything it was a perfect fit. As I was taking the ring off I felt my heart break. Yes the salesman was still holding on to the one that I wanted, but Clifton looked at him and said "You can put that back" she's going to take this one right here. That damn clearance case! I finally came to terms with the fact that I could not get the ring that I wanted so I sat back down at the clearance case and settled for the ring that Clifton picked.

Yes I was a little disappointed but happy all the same. After trying on the ring that Clifton picked Simone and I got up and walked out of the store and went into the shoe store next door. I turned to Simone and said "Girl your daddy is cheap" Simone laughed and said "yeah he is.

He could have gotten you the one you really wanted" I laughed and said "That's ok I got some words for him when we get home".

Christmas Morning I got up early because I knew that Clifton had to take Simone home and plus he had to work a half day. Keyonta was already up, and oh how I love my son. No matter how old he gets he always makes Christmas worth wild for me. He turned the living room lights on and as I walked in he said "Merry Christmas! Then asked "Mom should I wake Cliff? He should be in here with us to".

I guess Cliff heard what Keyonta said because as I was coming out of Simone's room he was dragging himself to the living room. We handed the kids their gifts, Simone was shocked because she had her IPOD that her dad was pretending to look for on Christmas Eve, and she also had clothes and other stuff as well. Keyonta was pretty pleased with his gifts and of course good old Cliff gave him money his usual. My enjoyment came when it was time for Clifton to open his gifts. I couldn't resist but I waited patiently as I handed him his things. I handed him all the gifts that were from the kids then lastly I handed him my gifts. He opened the first two boxes and found a robe that he said he wanted inside of one, and a pair of jeans and a shirt in the other. I handed him the last box and just waited with a small smile. Clifton tore the paper off the box all neat. I said to him "Baby tear that darn paper I only paid a dollar for it and its going in the garbage anyway, so hurry up and open it". When he opened that box and saw that it was the BOOTS he wanted, he couldn't believe it. He just smiled and said "Sweetheart how did you know? How did you find them? I have been looking for these in my size (15 I might add) for a while now. Aw man, man I can't believe you got these".

I just smiled and said "Yes I did that" and patted myself on the shoulder then said "I have ways of doing stuff to you know, did you forget who I am". He hugged me so tight and yes it really felt so good. Everybody was happy and that was the best Christmas gift for me. After everyone opened their things Simone said to her dad "Are you going to give Trice her present?" I looked over at her and said "Honey don't worry about that I already know what it is so it really doesn't matter". So while I am under the tree straightening other gifts and making sure the kids had all of their stuff Cliff comes back into the living room with this Kay's box, looks at my son and says "Keyonta with your permission may I have your mother's hand in marriage". I couldn't move; I was in total shock. I placed my hand over my mouth and moved slowly away from the Christmas tree. A small tear began to stream down my cheek as I turned to look at him. Clifton opened the box and Keyonta said "Pops you have my permission" then Clifton turned to me and said "Trice will you do me the honor of being my wife, will you marry me?" I looked at the box and to my surprise it was the ring that I wanted. Breathless and still tearing I said Yes, Cliff I will. I hugged and kissed him and he placed my ring on my finger. Simone was cheering in the back and Keyonta said "That's what's up, but pops what took you so long". We all laughed and Simone said I can't wait for the wedding.

That was the happiest and one of the proudest days of my life. I felt like Cinderella once prince charming found her again. Clifton asked me to be his wife with our children present and for him to ask my son of all people and my son say "Yes you have my permission." Trust me when I say that only GOD can give you treasures like that and that morning, the 25th day of December 2011 he most definitely gave me something more precious than silver or gold. Clifton and I were on top of the world. I called my mother still crying and of course she started crying. Cliff called his mother and his sister. His mother said to me "Congratulations Honey, I am so happy for you, I am happy for the both of you". My sister-in-law Nicole said "Alright now you are officially a part of the family and I am sorry that it took my damn brother so long". I don't know if Clifton knew, but at that moment he gave me back my happily ever after and that day will always be one that I will NEVER EVER FORGET!!

After he dropped Simone off at home he went to work. From what I heard he came in with a huge smile and shinning according to some of his partners. They all asked what was wrong. I also heard that he lost a bet and had to pay up. The bet was that he was going to be the next one to tie the knot and for a long time he denied it, but Christmas day he had to pay. One of our neighbors even told me that he smiled from ear to ear when he told him that he was about to get married. Our neighbor said to him "Man congratulations! But I've been there and done that. As a matter of fact I did it for 20 years" and he said that Clifton said "Oh yeah 20, well I'm going to out do you I'm going for a lifetime".

My lifetime cut short, my breathe taken away

Excitement and joy filled the Lewis household. Just to look at Clifton made me smiled. I don't know what it was about him but he kept a smile on my face. It was hard for me to be angry with him even when he would do something to work my nerve. I remember one day he came in from work and he was so charged. I looked at him and said "how may energy drinks have you had?" He smiled and said none then he started patting himself on the shoulder. So I asked "then what have you had?" He laughed and said Ms. Tucker, I mean soon to be Mrs. Lewis you listen and listen well, believe me when I tell you that my name is going to go down in history everybody is going to know who Clifton P. Lewis is". Of course I had to throw something smart into his mist of feeling himself. You are right, everyone will know who Clifton P. Lewis is because Tamara L. Tucker (Lewis) will soon be his wife so who wouldn't know who you are, look at the DIVA who'll always be by your side".

Clifton laughed and said "Woman please you have nothing to do with this". He then went on to tell me what happen at work that day that brought him home so amped up. Later on that evening I guess he told Keyonta the same story because all I heard was "Pops what! You the man if you are doing big things like that!" For three days my life was perfect I had everything that I had always dreamed I would have, my Fiancée' and the love of my life (soon to be my husband), my son and my daughter, a new home, and just pure happiness all over me. Nothing could take me off the high I was on.

The morning of Thursday December 29th everything was fine. I got up to get ready for work. I informed Clifton that we had to get the rest of the stuff out of the apartment because I wanted to give my former landlord the keys back. He told me that was fine because he was off which was even better because I had scheduled for us to pay a visit to the hall to place a deposit down for our October wedding. Clifton had no idea that I had done this but I was prepared to face the rapture of Cliff later. I knew he was going to have a fit but oh well wouldn't have been the first and it wasn't supposed to be the last.

I called Clifton around 3:30 that evening to see what was for dinner. I also told him that I would be leaving work at 4:30 so I wanted him and Keyonta to meet me over at the apartment building so we could finish up. As I asked Cliff and Keyonta met me and my mother at the apartment. My mom and I had already gathered the rest of what needed to be either taken to the alley or to good will. While we were finishing up Clifton informed me that he had to work his part-time job he said he forgot to tell me that he was called and asked if he could work because someone else had called off.

I looked at him and informed him that I had made plans for us. I knew that he was about to rip into me because I didn't tell him earlier. "Sweetheart why you didn't tell me this earlier" and what have I told you about making plans without telling me in advance." Well I didn't tell you because I knew you didn't have to work so it shouldn't have been an issue. "Where were we supposed to be going" was his question to me. With a little attitude in my voice, I said "We were supposed to go over to the hall to speak with them about the wedding". Clifton dropped the bag he was holding and said "Trice again why didn't you tell me this when I talk with you earlier today"?

I didn't feel like going back and forth with him so I said "Cliff forget it. I can re-schedule for another day". He looked at me like he really wanted to strangle me. He then said "see if they will let us come tomorrow". As he grabbed the bag he dropped he said "girl I don't know what I'm going to do with you, you don't listen. Sweetheart I have told you time after time you never know when I might be called in". "Called in for CPD business is one thing, but it's not like you're contractually committed to these darn side jobs". I said as I rolled my eyes. As we continued getting things together I started to feel sick. I don't know what it was but all of a sudden but my stomach began to turn, my head began to hurt, and my chest started to feel tight. I thought maybe it came from the dust because we were sweeping and mopping so I thought nothing of it and continued putting stuff inside of garbage bags.

My mom stated that she was getting tired so we decided that we would wrap everything up. Cliff and Keyonta took a few more things out to the garbage and we also load a few things into Cliff's car. That sick feeling seemed like it was getting worse and worse. Clifton told me that we had to hurry up because he was running late for work. As we all parted ways, Cliff kissed me and said "sweetheart I'll see you later". My mom went home, Keyonta and I were headed home, and Cliff went to work.

On our way home Keyonta looked at me and said "Mom you really don't feel good do you?" I told him that I didn't and I didn't know what was going on with me. I was fine earlier that day but again I just thought that this sick feeling came about because we were cleaning the apartment and maybe that could have triggered my asthma but all of a sudden like that, something just wasn't right.

Keyonta and I stopped to get dinner that night. When we finally got home I told Keyonta that I had to lay down. Before heading to bed I made Cliff's plate and placed it in the oven. About 7:30 that evening I called Clifton and said "Cliff I think you need to come home because I feel terrible my chest is really tight, my head is hurting, babe I don't know what's going on". Clifton said to me in his usual nonchalant voice "Sweetheart it's just your asthma take some of your inhaler, then look in the bathroom and take on of those cold and sinus pills. I'll bring some orange juice home and if you are not feeling better when I get there I'll take you to the ER". I thought to myself why is he not listening I want him to come home **NOW!** He also said to me "plus Keyonta is there with you and if you need to go to the E.R. before I get there he can take you." "Fine Cliff, your plate in the oven so if I'm sleep when you come in just wake me and I will warm it up for you". That would be the last time I would here Clifton's voice.

About 8:45 on the night of December 29, 2011 I was laying down, Keyonta was in the living room playing the game when I hear "mom it's a lot of police in the front yard". Half sleep half-awake I say to Keyonta what?

Keyonta then says "Mom I think you should get up because it's all a lot of police in the front yard and now they're coming to the door". I kind of sat up in the bed and said to Keyonta "Maybe somebody threw something in the yard and they are looking for it."

Two officers approached the front door of our home one of them knocked on the window. When they knocked Keyonta said "Mom please get up there knocking on the window now". Trembling I got out of the bed walked slowly into the living room as Keyonta opened the door for the officers. The male officer stood in the background, while the female officer calmly said "Latrice" and I said yes, she said "Honey you need to come with us right away Clifton been shot".

I couldn't move and I didn't understand what she was saying, it sounded like she was talking another language to me. I turned to Keyonta and said "what did she just say"?

My baby grab me and said "mom go get your shoes we have to go she said that Cliff been shot. Looking at the male officer that accompany the female officer I could not think positive I couldn't think of anything but OH MY GOD, PLEASE, PLEASE LET HIM BE OKAY. Tears began to stream down my face as my son escorted me to the police car. Lights and sirens were going and I could do nothing but cry my son held my hand and said "Mom it's going to be okay he'll be all right".

About time we got to the hospital there were so many police standing outside crying. At that moment my heart my, my soul, all that I had in me left. His partner Calvin grabbed me. He took me into this room set beside me in the chair. All I could do was look at him and say "Calvin please let me see him, go to tell him I'm here". With tears streaming down his face he said to me "Latrice I can't, I can't. "What do you mean you can't I don't understand".

Calvin held my hand so tight and said to me I can't. My family were all at the hospital with me, I was yelling somebody please call his mother, call his mom. Keyonta called Michael Clifton's Nephew and the next thing I saw was a doctor heading towards me, he kneeled in front of me grab my hands and said to me " we did everything we could I'm sorry" I screamed NO, NO! My son ran out of the room, out of the hospital. The last thing I remember was Superintendent McCarthy talking to me, and then awaking to an oxygen mask over my face and doctors and nurses standing all around me.

After coming to the realization of what just happened I kept asking "Where is his mom, where is my mother-in-law, please take me to his mom". I was informed that Nicole (my sister-in-law) was outside. They then took me to where mom Maxine was. They told me she had experienced chest pains. When I saw her lying in that bed with things attached to her, my heart wanted to stop. Trying to dry up my tears I grabbed her hand and said to her "Momma what am I going to do? What am I suppose to do"? She said to me "Oh baby, Honey" and then wiped my face. There were policemen and a few of the police Chaplin's ministers in the room with Mom Maxine and I. I guess after they knew that mom Maxine was ok they asked us if we were ready to see Clifton.

As we were being escorted to where they had Clifton laying I kept praying that this was all a nightmare and I was going to wake up and this joke will be over but once they got us to where he was my nightmare was real. My legs were weak, my entire insides shivering; as I approached the lifeless body of the love of my life. With mom Maxine on one side and I on the other I Say "Clifton you can't do this to me, please baby get up, you can't do this to me" please Cliff

I'm begging you, baby get up, I love you so much please just get up".

To hear the words his mother spoke that night are words that no mother should ever have to let come out of her mouth. "Baby you were supposed to bury me; I should be the one laying here not you. Clifton you were supposed to bury me, honey it's not suppose to be this way I should be laying there, Lord it should be me not my baby, Lord it should be me". There I was standing beside my mother-in-law helpless, my mind not even in the right state, my heart broken and my soul lost. The life that I knew was over, gone, taken away from me.

After allowing us time with Clifton Mom Maxine and I was escorted out. Along with the rest of our family we watched as Clifton was being taken away. His partners and fellow co-worker watching as well and like me they were still stuck at the question why? With Keyonta by my side and tears not stopping, I leaned against his arm and told him that I was not ready to say goodbye, how could this happen? I am not ready, I can't. My son said to me in tears as he hugged me "Mom they killed my dad, they took my pops away from me".

Clifton had always told me about his two other sisters. He spoke of the often so when I asked "When am I going to meet them?" Cliff being the procrastinator always said "Sweetheart soon you'll meet them soon". I met my other sister in-laws Matasha and LaShana a day after Clifton passed away. These two ladies embraced me and my son as if we had known each other our entire lives. It was an awesome experience meeting his (my) sisters that I heard so much about. In the mist of my tragedy I gained so much more.

I hate that we had to meet under such tragic conditions but as that old saying goes God knows when to place people in your life. During this time I also met Clifton's father Mr. Clifton Lewis Sr. I also met so many other people that knew Cliff and who loved and embraced just as I did.

The next two weeks was the toughest two weeks I have ever had to endure. It was like déjà vu. I just did this a year earlier with my brother and now I had to lay to rest the person that made my life complete, the person who gave me the world with 4 simple words, **"will you marry me"**. How is it that I went from the excitement and happiness of planning my dream wedding, to planning my husband to be funeral? How did my happily ever be taken away from me again, but this time it was not because of something he or I did.

Clifton and I were supposed to grow old together, we had a lot more fussing and disagreeing to do, we had vacations to go on, more proms and graduations to attend. When the time came, I had plans on leaving all the grandbabies on Grandpa Cliff while Grandma Trice did some shopping. This was not real; how could everything I had be taken away from me, my heart ripped from my chest and the love of my life I was now without. I was supposed to have **A LIFETIME!**

The morning of January 5, 2012 I along with Clifton's mother Maxine, Clifton father Clifton Sr, Clifton's (my) sisters Nicole, Matasha and Lashana, his (our) daughter Simone and my (our) son Keyonta and the rest of our families, Clifton partner Calvin, along with the rest of his brother and sisters of the tactical team and the entire 15th district, and the brotherhood of the entire Chicago Police Department and the world paid tribute to a man who's heart was filled with love, whose life was about serving and protecting, and whose spirit and laughter could fill a room in a matter of seconds. Who was big in size but small in conflict and always willing to lend a helping hand along with a kind word of advice and whose heart was just as big as the person who was carrying it.

It was cold that day but to the people that Clifton touched and helped throughout his life time; the chill of that day, of that moment was ignored. Hundreds of people lined the streets, filled United Baptist Church and maybe even set in front of a television. Officers from all over lined the streets standing at attention with heavy hearts but hands saluting to pay tribute to one of their own. To celebrate and remember **MY LOVE, MY LIFE, MY BEST FRIEND.**

Chicago Police Officer Clifton P. Lewis

END OF WATCH 29 DECEMBER, 2011

The love of my life

This picture was taken

December 25, 2011

After I said yes to become

Mrs. Clifton P Lewis

Made in the USA
Middletown, DE
27 May 2015